Brian Warrington

THE PRICE OF
TRUST

HOW COMPANIES AND PEOPLE ARE DESTROYED
BY WHITE-COLLAR CRIME

Brian Warrington

THE PRICE OF TRUST

HOW COMPANIES AND PEOPLE ARE DESTROYED BY WHITE-COLLAR CRIME

MEREO
Cirencester

Mereo Books

1A The Wool Market Dyer Street Cirencester Gloucestershire GL7 2PR
An imprint of Memoirs Publishing www.mereobooks.com

The price of trust: 978-1-86151-103-4

First published in Great Britain in 2014
by Mereo Books, an imprint of Memoirs Publishing

Copyright ©2014

The address for Memoirs Publishing Group Limited can be found at
www.memoirspublishing.com

The Memoirs Publishing Group Ltd Reg. No. 7834348

The Memoirs Publishing Group supports both The Forest Stewardship Council® (FSC®) and
the PEFC® leading international forest-certification organisations. Our books carrying both the
FSC label and the PEFC® and are printed on FSC®-certified paper. FSC® is the only
forest-certification scheme supported by the leading environmental organisations including
Greenpeace. Our paper procurement policy can be found at
www.memoirspublishing.com/environment

Typeset in 11.5/16pt Plantin
by Wiltshire Associates Publisher Services Ltd. Printed and bound in Great Britain by
Printondemand-Worldwide, Peterborough PE2 6XD

'To find out if you can trust someone, trust them'
Ernest Hemingway

'Love all, trust a few, do wrong to none'
William Shakespeare

Contents

Preface

Occupational fraud is growing rapidly, not only in the UK but around the globe. Numerous accounting company surveys on occupational fraud are carried out on a regular basis. These surveys mainly look at the financial implications and put forward estimates as to the cost to the economy of this growing problem. These surveys whilst being useful in general terms are in the main analysing reported and prosecuted occupational fraud.

One additional survey carried out in 2007 by KPMG deviated from the standard survey and looked at the profile of the typical occupational fraudster. This survey whilst being a useful additional contribution to knowledge, did not examine the pyschopathy or early warning signs.

The author of this book carried out original research prompted by the belief that the behaviour patterns of fraudsters would indicate personality disorders and that analysis of observed behaviour might reveal early warning signs. In his research he discovered that many of the perpetrators in the victim companies that were investigated showed behaviour patterns which would indicate the presence of personality disorders, particular, Narcissistic Personality Disorder (NPD), Anti-Social Personality Disorder (ASPD) and the Psychopath (Sociopath). Early warning signs were present in one hundred percent of the companies investigated; they were however not recognised by management.

If companies could be educated to recognise early warning signs, maybe ultimately, company directors could help to reduce the incidence of occupational fraud and save their companies from becoming victims of this growing problem. This author examines the psychopathy of perpetrators and shows the usefulness of companies being aware of the early warning signs which are always present. The book looks at the behaviour characteristics of perpetrators prior to discovery. including signs that would be looked for by industrial psychologists and more importantly company signs.

The victims of occupational fraud are often not seen as victims. For example, where perpetrators are prosecuted they are treated simply as witnesses in courts. Sentences are quite often not commensurate with the crime, judges believing that 'no one was hurt'. In fact many victims including relatives of the perpetrators suffer lasting psychological damage and stress induced medical conditions.

White-collar crime such as occupational fraud is in the main carried out by well-educated and qualified individuals, and is not gender specific.

The author will identify many of the methods used by occupational fraudsters and discuss the use of relatively simple indicator tools which if used could help to identify possible problems with employees.

Above all the reader will see that the Price of Trust is much more than the money lost to greedy fraudsters. The Betrayal of Trust in business can be and often is a traumatic event to the businessman. The psychological and emotional damage caused by such events is often life changing.

Some years ago the author was instrumental in discovering a case of occupational fraud. This was after he had accepted a position as chairman of a medium sized UK company. Following the dismissal of the perpetrator and many conversations with the auditor's forensic team he decided to research occupational fraud. This subject appeared to be somewhat neglected by academic researchers. His initial requirement was to investigate the Incidence of psychopathy and early warning signs in victim companies of occupational fraud.

During the time when the auditors' forensic team was in house and in subsequent discussions with the directors of the business, it became apparent that there had been, over a period of several years, incidents which with hindsight could be described as early warning signs. These signs had not been appreciated. The finance director who had perpetrated the crime had served with the company for some twenty years and been totally trusted. He was diagnosed by a criminal psychologist as exhibiting the characteristic traits of Narcissistic Personality Disorder at severe level.

The author subsequently added the requirement to investigate the psychological stress and emotional turmoil to victims caused by the traumatic event of fraud discovery. Such victims included directors, senior managers, company owners and directors of large public companies and also colleagues of the perpetrators.

Introduction

Enron and World Com in the US, the Mirror Group in the UK and the ensuing law suits have brought the subject of corporate fraud more into the public eye than any previous business scandals. Unfortunately corporate crime is increasing both in the US and Europe. According to the FBI, employee fraud is the fastest growing crime in the US. As with many things, trends in the US tend to be followed in the UK (Buchanan-Cook, D. (2006) 'Fraud -The threat from within', UK Law journal of Scotland).

The British Chamber of Commerce is reporting that an estimated 20% of small businesses in the UK fail due to internal theft and fraud (BCC). Not all corporate fraud is occupational fraud, the subject of this book. Occupational fraud, stealing from one's employer, is on the increase across the globe. By definition stealing from one's employer covers not only stealing cash but assets and benefits. Assets are sold and converted to cash or simply used by the fraudster, for example computer equipment, spare parts, media, mobile phones etc - the list is endless. The ever more materialistic society in which we live and the decline in moral values coupled with the concept that 'It's OK to steal from your employer' would seem to be core reasons why occupational fraud is on the increase.

STAFF FRAUD SURVEYS

Several surveys have been conducted on this subject in an

effort to further understand the reasons why people steal from their employers. In 1999 Michael G Kessler & Associates carried out an 'exhaustive study' by surveying 500 employees nationwide in the USA. These results astounded business owners and management level employees.

'The results showed that extreme employee loyalty may in fact be a guise to extreme employee dishonesty. Employees that appeared to have the company's best interest in the forefront of their activities were often just using this ploy to steal from the company' - Kessler, M G & Associates (1999)

Kessler discovered that employee fraud outstrips shoplifting theft. They further submit that employee fraud is the cause of business failure in one out of three businesses in the States. This study showed that 79% of employees stole from their employer. It further stated that 21% of employees are basically honest and would never steal from their employer. Unfortunately it also showed that 13% were dishonest and would undoubtedly attempt theft, while the remaining 66% would steal if they saw others doing it without repercussions.

When discussing the reasons why employees steal, the following reasons were given:

49% steal due solely to greed.

43% steal due to vindictiveness or the need to get even for poor treatment. This includes the need to get even with their boss or firm for injustices thrust on them.

8% steal out of need.

Kessler makes a further interesting comment: 'The easiest way for an employee to perpetrate the theft is by a show of extreme loyalty' - Kessler, M G & Associates (1999)

In the UK a similar survey was carried out by employment law consultancy Peninsula. This survey found that 72% of office workers in the UK admitted stealing from their employer more than once.

'Contrary to these findings, however, more than 81% of those who stole said that they believed stealing to be morally wrong' (Peninsula 2007).

A further UK survey was carried out by researchers at Keele University in the UK. They polled 1807 people in England and Wales 61% of whom admitted to one of a series of offences ranging from paying cash in hand to keeping money when given too much change and stealing from work. Whilst this survey was looking at middle class crime and theft it makes some useful comments regarding employee fraud and attitudes. The author of this research, Professor Suzanne Karstedt, said: 'Contempt for the law is as widespread in the centre of society as it is assumed to be rampant among specific marginal groups... Anti-Social behaviour by the few is mirrored by anti-civil behaviour by the many' (Karstedt S. 2007).

This research also states that a large number of offenders in the poll were classified as middle class and 'respectable' by the academics. This modern research would certainly endorse the white-collar crime description attached to perpetrators of occupational fraud. Keele's researchers make the following pointed comment:

'It's obvious, then, that the law-abiding majority is a

myth and we really are a nation of Fagins. Even if the pockets we're picking happen to be those of the people paying our wages.' (Karstedt S, 2007)

This type of thinking as described in such surveys is in the same vein as overstating insurance claims. Many so-called normal people seem to take the attitude that it's OK to inflate an insurance loss because no one gets hurt. In reality everyone who buys insurance gets hurt because, with inflated claims, premiums go up. What type of person commits occupation fraud? And what are the reasons? Is there a profile for the employee fraudster?

PROFILE OF A FRAUDSTER

In 2007 KPMG deviated from their normal fraud survey to look at the profile of fraudsters. They stated that the typical fraudster was aged between 35 and 55; this age group represented 70% of identified fraudsters:

'By the time he has started enriching himself by illegal means, he has usually been employed by the company for six or more years. He typically works in the finance department and commits the fraud single-handed. In 86% of cases he is management - and in two thirds of cases he is a member of senior management. Greed and opportunity are his motivating factors.' (KPMG 2007)

KPMG further report that 60% of frauds are carried out by senior management, sometimes board directors, and 68% operate independently.

The internal occupational fraudster most often works in the finance department, followed by operations and sales departments. Sometimes the CEO himself is the perpetrator. Misappropriation of money was revealed by KPMG to be the most common type of fraud. More pertinent, and borne out by the author's research, is the fact that 91% of perpetrators did not stop at one transaction; further, one in three fraudsters acted in excess of fifty times. KPMG attest that greed and opportunity when taken together account for 73% of the profiles. In 49% of cases reviewed, the fraudsters exploited weak internal controls. This was borne out many times during the author's research. It is also reported by KPMG that most business sectors are affected by white-collar crime, the exceptions with a lower incidence being the chemical, pharmaceutical and biotech sector.

LEARNING FROM FRAUDSTERS

Martin Gill, in his paper Learning from Fraudsters, reports on his interviews with jailed offenders. He interviewed perpetrators who had stolen between £65,000 and an estimated £25 million. Gill quotes NCIS (National Criminal investigation Service), who estimated that in 2004 the cost to the UK economy of fraud in listed companies was £14 billion.

In Learning from Fraudsters, several of the convicted fraudsters interviewed maintained that they could easily fool auditors, as they only audited numbers and paid little or no attention to systems. One of the fraudsters interviewed stated 'I could run rings round them'. He was referring to a quality company which was his company's auditor. He further stated:

'Auditors can only work on figures they have got, audit

the same. Auditors came to me and I just lied to them and gave them false pieces of paper and that was that. The checking process was abysmal; I was not worried because I have twenty years' experience of auditors.'

All of Gill's interviewees had been convicted of fraud, theft or deception; sentences passed by the courts had been between 21 months and seven years. The age of these criminals ranged from 24 to 62 years (Gill M 2004).

For the same period, Norwich Union estimated the cost to be £16 billion (NU 2004). Both these estimates cover all fraud and not just occupational fraud, the subject of this book.

Is there an economic need to steal, for example to feed a drug addiction, pay a gambling debt or finance a lifestyle? Norwich Union further summarises the problem in the UK:

'Fraud is not a victimless crime. It appears as such because it lacks visibility and its scale is not understood. Constraints upon the police translate into a perceived reticence to prosecute fraudsters, sustaining the widely-held view that fraud is not a real crime in the same way burglary or theft are considered to be. Prosecution levels for fraud in the UK are low, and in the event of a conviction being achieved, the likelihood of strong sentencing is also low. This absence of effective deterrents to committing fraud is a significant factor in its growth, and increased exploitation by organised crime. The National Criminal Intelligence Service (NCIS) has estimated that 'UK organised crime now earns as much from fraud as from drugs' (NU 2004).

More disturbing is the lack of official policies in the UK

to combat the increasing trend of occupational fraud. Norwich Union further suggests the involvement of organised crime:

'The proceeds of fraud are fuelling the growth of organised crime. The UK does not have a published and clearly articulated national strategy on fraud, and no comprehensive official annual national statistics are captured or trends projected' (NU 2004).

White-collar crime

Occupational fraud, in general terms, can be referred to as white-collar crime.

It is now more than seventy years since Edwin Sutherland coined the phrase, in an address in 1939 to the American Sociological Society at Indiana University. Sutherland's objective, although thought by many to be politically biased, at least made academics and researchers look at the middle and upper classes, people who were educated and well qualified and were often working in large organisations as well as government departments.

White-collar crime covers many crimes, only one of which is stealing from your employer and covering this up by falsifying company accounts. Others defined by Sutherland include embezzlement, restraint of trade and rebates to some customers but not all. Also included are patents and copyright and trademark infringements, along with misrepresentation in advertising. Unfair labour practices, financial manipulations and some war crimes are also listed by Sutherland. He also refers to financial manipulations by companies and/or their executives as fraud or violation of trust. He states that these crimes include embezzlement, extortionate salaries and bonuses and other misapplication of corporate funds in the interests of executives or of holders of certain securities. Fraud in the sale of securities includes public misrepresentation in the form of stock market manipulations. Sutherland also includes in his definitions of white-collar crime inflation of capital and inadequate or misleading financial reports, and other manipulations (Sutherland 1983).

Sutherland covered many other sub-divisions of the above, but was very scathing about embezzlement, which is, in the context of this book, occupational fraud:

'The ordinary case of embezzlement is a crime by a single individual in a subordinate position against a strong corporation. It is therefore the most foolish of white-collar crimes' (Sutherland 1983).

Some modern cases where executives at the very top of corporations commit white-collar crime would seem to be at odds with the above comment from Sutherland. One such case is the Robert Maxwell scandal. Enron in the United States, along with World Com, are more examples where the very top executives became perpetrators.

Over the years since Sutherland coined the phrase, much has been written on the subject of white-collar crime yet very little specifically on occupational fraud. Some papers and books have also been written on the subject of victims of white-collar crime.

Very little research has been carried out into victims of occupational fraud. Many of the papers written on victims in both of these headings are literature reviews. There are however some empirical research papers which have used interviews with victims as the method of investigation. Also there have been papers written that to a degree criticise Sutherland's work, maintaining it was politically biased. One such paper, The Sociological Origins of White-collar Crime by John S. Baker Jr, states:

'The rules of criminal intent and presumption of innocence... are not required in all prosecution in criminal courts and the number of exceptions authorized by statutes is increasing. If nothing else, his disregard for age-old foundational principles of criminal law should cast doubt on the balance of Sutherland's work. Sutherland goes on to construct a class-based definition of white-collar crime. He is concerned with who the alleged perpetrator was, rather than what that person might have done. White-collar crime, says Sutherland, is crime committed by a person of respectability and high social status in the course of his occupation. With this radical redefinition, Sutherland attempted to drain the word 'crime' of its meaning. He made distinctions not on the basis of an act or intent, but according to the status of the accused. Sutherland's supporters have stated: 'The term white-collar crime served to focus attention on the social position of the perpetrators and added a bite to commentaries about the illegal acts of businessmen, professionals, and politicians that is notably absent in the blander designations, such as occupational crime and economic crime, that sometimes are employed to refer to the same kinds of lawbreaking'. Even his friends acknowledged that Sutherland was intent upon pressing a political viewpoint and that he did so in a tone... reminiscent of the preaching of outraged biblical prophets.' (Baker J S 2004)

Controversial as Sutherland's words were in his 1949 original book, the fact remains that the term is still widely used and sentences handed down for such criminals here in the UK and in the US are believed by many to be too lenient (BDO 2006).

By applying the term to people in positions of responsibility, there has to be a violation of the trust given to such persons. Where the crime committed by white-collar criminals is for personal gain as opposed to manipulating balance sheets etc. for corporate benefit, there is the opportunity to steal without violence or burglary. No one would suggest that burglars and people who steal using violence are white-collar criminals and therefore Sutherland's term assumes that the perpetrators of such crimes are reasonably well-educated and well-qualified individuals. Often such criminals are senior managers and work in accounting departments. In many cases researched, these perpetrators in management violate the delegated trust that goes with the position. Such criminals are trusted with company assets and finances. As well as their acts of fraud, stealing company money and/or assets, they are legally in breach of their fiduciary duty to the company which employs them.

In order to investigate the feelings and welfare of victims of occupational fraud, there is a need to understand why the victims suffered. In many cases victims continue to suffer years after the trauma of discovering fraud. As owners, directors, managers, employees, shareholders and families of these groups, as well as families of perpetrators, they may all suffer emotionally, due in the main to the betrayal of trust. The discovery that the person they knew is not the person they thought they were but someone who was capable of stealing in many cases large sums of money is hard to understand and come to terms with. The betrayal of trust and all that it signifies is a fundamental betrayal (see chapter 5, Betrayal of Trust). Coming to terms with the discovery that a colleague, employee, husband, wife or family member is not what they appeared to be can and does cause in many victims a deep psychological hurt or damage.

It becomes necessary therefore to consider the character of the perpetrator and where possible any personality traits that may be indicated by their behavioural characteristics, personality flaws or disorders. In some of the cases researched by the author, management had been made aware for the first time of serious personality defects in the perpetrators. This was usually where perpetrators were reported to the authorities and subsequently jailed for their offence. This usually comes about when the defence lawyers request a psychiatric analysis in order to put up a defence on grounds of diminished responsibility. This rarely works, but it does put on record the presence (or not) of personality disorders.

Other cases where personality disorders have been noted include where there has been a divorce following the discovery of fraud, followed by subsequent feelings of betrayal. In these cases, where court-appointed psychologists or psychiatrists had diagnosed personality flaws, the fraudster (husband or wife) became extremely aggressive and threatening to his/her spouse. Restraining court orders had to be sought in order to safeguard the victims and their children. In all these cases there had been a diagnosis of personality defaults.

These revelations do nothing to modify the feelings of disgust and betrayal in the victim's eyes, quite the reverse in many cases. The discovery that they had been working with or married to, for example, a person suffering from a psychopathic personality disorder increases injury and hurt to the victims.

When taking these facts into consideration it becomes necessary to give consideration to the personality disorders reported as having been diagnosed by professionals. Some of the interviewed victims reported observed characteristics in the perpetrators that could indicate the presence of a personality disorder. There was no attempt to diagnose these perpetrators, because an impression from bitter managers, directors and owners after the event is a far cry from a diagnosis, nor was it in the remit of the author's research to diagnose.

Nevertheless, some credence has to be given when personality disorders have been diagnosed by professionals. This allows a better understanding of the emotional feelings and hurt suffered by victims. In Chapter Two there is a section on definitions which addresses personality disorders and more importantly the difficulties that psychiatrists and psychologists have in establishing a pure diagnosis.

The question remains as to the appropriateness of differentiating white-collar criminals and occupational fraudsters from other types of criminal. It is too simplistic to argue that they are of a higher social status and educational level than, shall we say, street criminals. Many so-called street criminals tend to be opportunistic and varied in their crimes, whereas occupational fraudsters undoubtedly plan not only their methods but their way of disguising their actions by falsifying company accounts.

David Jones discusses in some detail differences between the professional white-collar criminal and street criminals. When discussing criminal careers, Jones quotes from Weisburd et al (2001) on Piquero and Benson 2004: 'They argue that the pattern of offending characteristic of white-collar crime is very different from those crimes more typically captured by the longitudinal studies (which might be referred to as street crime). White-collar crime tends to be committed by those who first offend well into adulthood and who are likely to be middle-class and relatively well educated'.

Weisburd et al (2001) suggest that this is a major problem for criminal career theorists:

'There are a couple of objectives to this analysis, first empirical evidence on the childhood and family backgrounds of white-collar criminals had not being gathered. It is possible that the lives of such offenders have been marked by antisocial behaviour and possibly family deprivation before adulthood; second, it may be that some similarity with patterns of street crime does emerge when the distinction is made between chronic and one off offenders.'

'However, Weisburd 'found that 'chronic white-collar offenders did not seem so different from more serious general offenders, deviance in the lives of those offenders is not restricted to criminality, but often appears to be the central part of their childhood development and adult histories such offenders are well described by common crime samples' (Jones 2008, p.100)

This author's research did not look into the backgrounds of occupational fraudsters, neither were they discussed with interviewees. It was apparent that the corporate fraudsters investigated carried out their crimes on many occasions and used more than one fraudulent method over a period of years. The more devious ones were getting involved with many different devious practices and accounting system manipulation. In several of the cases researched there was evidence of having committed occupational fraud previously in other companies and in two cases following the case being investigated, in their new jobs?

REGULATORY MATTERS

'The sentencing of white-collar offenders is an important part of regulation because the prospect of meaningful sanctions is crucial for deterrence and punishment and also reflects moral condemnation of activities. Although sentences for white-collar offenders attract less public attention than those for conventional criminals, they do attract criticism where, for example, serious fraudsters receive short prison sentences or companies blamed for deaths or injuries are given a relatively small fine. They are often described as 'paltry' and criticisms reflect concerns that they undermine the deterrent power of the law and are 'unfair', considering the harm that has been done. Sentencing raises similar issues to those encountered in relation to law and its enforcement. Its assumed lack of severity is often cited as one of the major features of white-collar crime and is popularly and academically thought to result from the high class of offenders'. (Croall 2001a, p.122.)

Many companies try to regulate the incidence of fraud by internal measures. Large companies have internal audit staff and some small and medium size companies have anti-fraud measures in place. Unfortunately in many of the cases investigated such measures were not monitored, making them useless. Croall endorses these statistics and states:

'Many crimes are not reported, leading to a large 'dark' or 'hidden' figure, and, in what has been described as a process of attrition, only a small proportion of reports are investigated by the police, 'counted' as offences and result in a conviction. These are supplemented by a large number of alternative sources - victim surveys and crime 'audits' cast some light on the hidden figure, although they too leave out some offences.'

It becomes clear that investigating victims of white-collar crime and occupational fraud is a much-neglected subject. There are many more victim groups who suffer because of unscrupulous perpetrators. The hurt and damage caused goes further than the financial loss and hardship caused by such criminals. Psychological and emotional damage can be widespread following the discovery of fraud in companies. The concept of the loss only being financial is a myth. Many of the victims are not only the ones directly affected by monetary losses; families of victims and perpetrators' families suffer immeasurably, along with company owners and shareholders and in some cases employees.

The ultimate betrayal of trust is hard for victims to accept and in many cases the victims are in denial sometimes for many years; up to three years is not uncommon.

Defining occupational fraud

The Association of Certified Fraud Examiners defines occupational fraud as: 'The use of one's occupation for personal enrichment through the deliberate misuse or misapplication of the employing organization's resources or assets. This definition is very broad, encompassing a wide range of misconduct by employees, managers, and executives. Occupational fraud schemes can be as simple as pilferage of company supplies or as complex as sophisticated financial statement frauds. All occupational fraud schemes have four key elements in common. The activity: is clandestine; violates the perpetrator's fiduciary duties to the victim organization, is committed for the purpose of direct or indirect financial benefit to the perpetrator; and costs the employing organization assets, revenue or reserves' (ACFE 2006)

FRAUD

Fraud is a term that is used in many situations by the layman when discussing stealing or theft. When we look at the definition of occupational fraud above it serves a much better understanding. How does the law in the UK define fraud as applied to the subject of this research? The UK Fraud Act 2006 indicates that a person can be found guilty of fraud if he/she is in breach of any of the three sections listed:

(1) A person is guilty of fraud if he is in breach of any of the sections listed in subsection.

(2) (which provide for different ways of committing the offence).

(2) The sections are—

(a) section 2 (fraud by false representation),

(b) section 3 (fraud by failing to disclose information), and

(c) section 4 (fraud by abuse of position). (Fraud Act 2006)

In occupational fraud cases investigated, it could be argued that all three of the above are applicable. Section 4, fraud by abuse of position, covers occupational fraud implicitly, as it is the abuse of the fraudster's position and the betrayal of the trust of his/her position that makes the fraud possible.

The Fraud Act further defines section 4: Fraud by abuse of position.

(1)   A person is in breach of this section if he:

(a)   occupies a position in which he is expected to safeguard, or not to act against, the financial interests of another person,

(b)   dishonestly abuses that position, and

(c)   intends, by means of the abuse of that position—

(i)   to make a gain for himself or another, or

(ii)   to cause loss to another or to expose another to a risk of loss.

(2)   A person may be regarded as having abused his position even though his conduct consisted of an omission rather than an act. (Fraud Act 2006)

The Government fraud review overseen by Lord Goldsmith in 2006 further defines what is meant by fraud. Paragraph 4 of the excerpt below, Fraud by abuse of position, is particularly relevant to this research into occupational fraud. However both sections 2 and 3 are also relevant. Failure to disclose information as in section 3 along with section 2 dealing with false representation succinctly covers the issue of falsifying company records to cover up and attempt to hide stealing from companies by occupational fraudsters.

Excerpts from the Fraud Review 2006:

FRAUD BY FALSE REPRESENTATION

(1)   A person is in breach of this section if he:

(a)   dishonestly makes a false representation, and

(b)   intends, by making the representation:

(i)   to make a gain for himself or another, or

(ii)   to cause loss to another or to expose another to a risk of loss.

(2)   A representation is false if:

(a)   it is untrue or misleading, and

(b)   the person making it knows that it is, or might be, untrue or misleading.

(3)   'Representation' means any representation as to fact or law, including a representation as to the state of mind of:

(a)   the person making the representation, or

(b)   any other person.

(4)   A representation may be express or implied.

(5)   For the purposes of this section a representation may be regarded as made if it (or anything implying it) is submitted in any form to any system or device designed to receive, convey or respond to communications (with or without human intervention). Fraud by failing to disclose information.

A person is in breach of this section if he:

(a)   Dishonestly fails to disclose to another person information which he is under a legal duty to disclose, and

(b)   intends, by failing to disclose the information:

(i)   to make a gain for himself or another, or

(ii) to cause loss to another or to expose another to a risk of loss.

Fraud by abuse of position.

(1)   A person is in breach of this section if he:

(a)   occupies a position in which he is expected to safeguard, or not to act against, the financial interests of another person,

(b)   dishonestly abuses that position, and

(c)   intends, by means of the abuse of that position:

(i)   to make a gain for himself or another, or

(ii) to cause loss to another or to expose another to a risk of loss.

(2)   A person may be regarded as having abused his position even though his conduct consisted of an omission rather than an act. (Fraud review 2006)

MORE FRAUD DEFINITIONS

The word 'fraud' is often used loosely, but not legally, to cover a whole variety of conduct associated with obtaining money by deception: embezzlement, plain stealing and malfeasance could also be used. Malfeasance would seem be an appropriate description for occupational fraud. Most perpetrators of this type of crime endeavour to cover their tracks by falsifying company records. Malfeasance, when applied to financial matters, is difficult to define. Broadly speaking it refers to illegally and intentionally doing something wrong involving dishonesty and covering up the crime by falsifying company records and exceeding authority for personal, pecuniary gain. The Legal Dictionary definition defines malfeasance as 'intentionally doing something either legally or morally wrong which one had no right to do. It always involves dishonesty, illegality, or knowingly exceeding authority for improper reasons'.

Pecuniary advantage or gain also needs a definition and can be found in the UK Theft Act 1968 (1996 amendment):

OBTAINING PECUNIARY ADVANTAGE BY DECEPTION

(1) A person who by any deception dishonestly obtains for himself or another any pecuniary advantage shall on conviction on indictment be liable to imprisonment for a term not exceeding five years.

(2) All cases in which a pecuniary advantage within the meaning of this section is to be regarded as obtained for a person are cases where-

(a) [Repealed];

(b) he is allowed to borrow by way of overdraft, or to take out any policy of insurance or annuity contract, or obtains an improvement of the terms on which he is allowed to do so; or

(c) he is given the opportunity to earn remuneration or greater remuneration in an office or employment, or to win money by betting.

(3) For purposes of this section 'deception' has the same meaning as in section 15 of this Act.

Malfeasance would therefore seem to be a fair description of occupational fraud as this type of fraud usually requires that company records are falsified to cover the fraudster's tracks. We can also define falsifying company records and accounting in section 17 of the Theft act:

False accounting.

'(1) Where a person dishonestly, with a view to gain for himself or another or with intent to cause loss to another,-

(a) destroys, defaces, conceals or falsifies any account or any record or document made or required for any accounting purpose; or

(b) in furnishing information for any purpose produces or makes use of any account, or any such record or document as aforesaid, which to his knowledge is or may be misleading, false or deceptive in a material particular; he shall, on conviction on indictment, be liable to imprisonment for a term not exceeding seven years'.

(2) For purposes of this section a person who makes or concurs in making in an account or other document an entry which is or may be misleading, false or deceptive in a material particular, or who omits or concurs in omitting a material particular from an account or other document, is to be treated as falsifying the account or document.' (HMSO 1996)

Perpetrators of malfeasance are usually in a position of trust in that because of their climb up the corporate ladder, they are in senior positions and thus have access. The betrayal of such trust is, not surprisingly, one of the main reasons why companies are reluctant to report corporate fraud. Management see this betrayal as a weakness in their managerial abilities. They are devastated when fraudsters in their organisation are exposed. They see this very much as a reflection on them, as they should have spotted oddities and acted. In some cases they did, but could not, or did not, have the ability to recognise what they had observed as an early warning sign.

In many cases the price paid for this trust causes deep emotional and psychological hurt. In short the price of trust can be high, both in monetary terms and the psychological damage to trusting managers.

Less than 50% of UK listed companies have effective anti-fraud measures in place (BDO 2005). The figure is undoubtedly considerably less in private companies; many small to medium-size UK companies cannot afford the staff overhead of initiating effective anti-fraud measures. More importantly, many do not even consider that there is a risk. However, Paul Babiak asserts: 'Almost four out of 10 business owners in Britain view the possibility of fraud - particularly being ripped off by one of their own employees - as being the biggest threat to their company' (CNN 2004).

Occupational fraud is undoubtedly a major problem to UK businesses. A very small percentage of cases are reported and the financial numbers in loss terms are getting larger each year for reported incidents.

BDO in its latest survey, contends that one of the main reasons for not reporting is the lack of confidence in the judiciary to pass adequate sentencing. The authors of the BDO Fraudtrack state: 'Our research showed a lack of confidence in the level of sentencing handed down to fraudsters. In 2005, the typical sentence for a fraudster taking £1M was under four years.' (BDO Fraudtrack 4)

Judges would appear to take the view that as no one has been hurt, there is not a requirement to hand down long sentences. They would appear to be ignoring the psychological and emotional damage caused by industrial psychopaths to their manager victims, not to mention the onset of latent medical conditions brought about by the stress levels endured.

In publicly-listed companies in the UK, there is a legal obligation to report financial irregularities, but in many cases ways are found to avoid the decision, usually because bad publicity is seen by the Board as a failure. In private companies without outside shareholders there is no legal requirement to report. If, however, the business ownership includes a non-active shareholder with 26% or more of the issued share capital, there is an obligation to report fraud (Companies House 2007).

Listed companies account for only about 0.13% of UK registered companies. There are approximately two million companies registered in the UK. Of this number there are 1234 listed on the stock exchange and a further 1348 listed on AIM, alternative investment market. The two million also include very small one-man convenience companies (Companies House 2007).

Various estimates from organisations conducting surveys into occupational fraud suggest that less than 10% of all corporate employee frauds are reported to the authorities. Even less are reported by financial institutions. One potential explanation for the financial institutions' reluctance to report victimisation is their reluctance to endure bad publicity, it becomes more desirable to take care of the problem internally by offsetting the losses against bad debt reserves and simply firing the perpetrator. Many financial institutes, banks and credit card companies in the US have reserves as much as15% of turnover. This figure is a balance sheet item quoted as bad debt provision. According to one US State attorney interviewed, this is where many internal frauds losses are posted. (Brock 2007) It is easy to understand therefore the very large estimates attributable to all economic crime.

Brief description of companies investigated

The descriptions of the companies researched is not exhaustive. It is a cross section to enable the reader to see the diversity of companies who became victims. Companies investigated in similar fields to the ones described have been omitted. The ones chosen to describe were identified so as to illustrate that no company or business sector is immune to occupational fraud. In order to maintain confidentially and anonymity, descriptions have been kept somewhat vague so as to ensure any reader would not be able to identify the specific company detailed.

COMPANY A

Located in the south of the UK, this company is a main motor car distributor. The owner founder, a chartered accountant, founded and managed the company. He had implemented several anti-fraud procedures. He knew from experience that the motor trade is, in his words, 'rife with fiddles'. As the company built up over many years he started to hire more expensive and capable people. One such person was a highly paid employee, employed as the service manager. The owner trusted the man, as he exhibited dedication, loyalty and a keenness to please. He noticed that the employee was always the first in each morning and the last to leave; he also often worked weekends without being asked. His first impression was that this man was a good employee and was very keen to please. He became suspicious after a while and one day whilst doing his accounts noticed some oddities. He challenged his service manager, who denied any wrong doing but became extremely aggressive. The owner brought in the police; the service manager was charged and went to court. He was found guilty of theft. This perpetrator exhibited many behavioural characteristics of personality disorder. The relatively low level of cash that the perpetrator stole did not cause the company any lasting problems.

COMPANY B

This Company is a group in the transport business, with several branches and two of the businesses had been bought. The company in which the fraud occurred was bought in the early 2000s, all staff members were kept on, and no one was made redundant. The transport manager of the acquired company was very soon made up to group director level. He was knowledgeable and hard-working, often arriving at work early and leaving late. He had worked for this company in excess of ten years. As is usual with companies, there was a PAYE audit early in 2006, carried out by the Inland Revenue. This type of audit is carried out on a random basis, not every year unless there are suspicions. It is routinely carried out every few years, but always within ten years of previous audits. After the first day the inspector became suspicious of time sheets on file for 'drivers' mates'. With large transporters there is a legal requirement for drivers always to have a 'mate' on board; this is to assist where necessary with reversing and unloading. The inspector informed the chief accountant that he was concerned that the time sheets were not tying up with payments or with the time sheets for the drivers. The transport manager/director was asked questions and apparently waffled and delayed in providing the information requested. Within a day or so sufficient evidence was uncovered to make it necessary for the chief accountant to look back through the files.

Following this investigation a pattern emerged. The transport manager had been filling out false drivers' mates timesheets. Sometimes they were legitimate names of people who had previously worked for the company, but bank accounts that BACS payment were made into were either the manager's own account or some of his family members' bank accounts. Following three days of investigation a board meeting was held and the board was split. Two wanted to fire the manager immediately, whereas the other two wanted, after interviewing the perpetrator, to give him another chance following admission and apology for his misdemeanours. He insisted that he had only being fiddling for a short period of time.

The chief accountant was one of the two voting for instant dismissal and informing the police. The accountant believed that the manager was lying. He spent a considerable amount of time going back through time sheet records for many years and in fact established a pattern.

A further board meeting was called and this time with the new evidence the perpetrator was dismissed following the mandatory disciplinary hearing. The police were called in and the manager was arrested. It became evident that the man in question had been to jail before for a similar crime some years before he joined the company. The court case was short after the perpetrator admitted over thirty cases of fraud. He would not admit to two charges which involved using his son's name and bank account. He was jailed for two years.

The total amount stolen is still unknown but the fraudster was jailed for stealing £60,000. The chief accountant believed that over a period of ten years he had probably got away with considerably more.

COMPANY C

This case is not a company in the strictest case; it is in fact, a registered charity operating in a relatively small geographical area. The charity was very well established and had grown over the last twenty years or so. Employees numbered between fifty and sixty at the time of the fraud. Following the resignation of the accountant, management employed the local office of a national recruitment and temporary staff agency to find a replacement accountant. An accountant was hired for a probationary period pending suitability. He was hard working and enthusiastic and was liked by many of the staff. He persuaded the charity to install a Sage accounting system, as the system currently in use had only the payroll computerised. This move was agreed with the Board of Trustees. The new recruit worked hard and installed Sage. He also trained the other members of the accounts department in its use. The accounts department and most of the trustees were not familiar with accounting and did not fully understand the accepted protocol of daily backup. The temporary accountant found it easy to persuade the team that accepted practice was to back up to a disk, which would be taken home each day, 'Just in case there is a fire.'

He continued to work hard following his appointment as a permanent staff member, always arriving early and leaving late and never taking holidays other than the odd day. After a few months the new accountant seemed to upset some of the staff who had previously liked him. He was felt to be manipulative and a bully. About eighteen months after his permanent staff appointment one of the junior accounts staff went to the Managing Director and insisted that there were anomalies on the payroll. The MD listened, but he was not particularly accountancy aware. He interviewed the new accountant, who managed to smooth-talk him, baffling him with jargon. The managing director bought his explanations. Things went back to normal.

Two or three months after this incident the managing director received a letter from a supplier. The letter enclosed a cheque, which apparently was a duplicate payment. Just why this supplier had decided to write to the MD is not known. The MD did some investigations using the staff member who had previously blown the whistle on the accountant. It was an easy matter to discover that there were several incidents of duplicate payments to various suppliers. The new accountant was suspended pending an investigation using the auditors. Shortly after the forensic accounting team came in the police were informed and the accountant was arrested.

During the lengthy investigation, there were two burglaries. Both involved the accounts department. On the first occasion, files were stolen. The second time the computer system was attacked and some records were erased. The police were not able to implicate the accountant. The problem now was, you cannot audit what is not there. Research was unable to determine the nature of the stolen files or the detail of computer erasures. It would appear that the accountant had planted a bug in the computer system, which caused the system to crash on a regular basis. Naturally he was always able to restore using his back-up disk. Following the arrest the system crashed as planned and he was not available to restore. The cost to the charity to rebuild their system was not insignificant.

There were two main frauds. One was duplicate payments to many suppliers. The other involved the accountant's salary; he had been paying himself about 25 per cent more each month than his agreed contractual salary. The whistle-blower was right. Following the court case the perpetrator was sent to jail and it was revealed that he had been to jail previously for fraud in a town several hundred miles away. This charity did have some anti-fraud policies in place but they were not operated correctly or monitored.

COMPANY D

This company was a specialist company in networking and security. The company operated mainly with organisations in the medium to large sector of business. It had been established in the seventies and had grown to be a respectable and well-known company in the IT services sector. They employed around seventy people, excluding contractors and temporary staff. Since originally breaking even after a couple of years' trading the company had increases its profit base over the years and because of the mix of products and services had maintained good margins over many years.

This company was the only one in this research where the owner and Managing Director agreed to the researcher interviewing staff lower than board level. It is also the largest of the companies investigated that went out of business because of the cash-flow problems caused by the fraud. This happened about six months after the MD had agreed to be interviewed.

In total three of the companies researched went down due to unscrupulous occupational fraudsters. The other two were company H and Company K. Of further interest to this research is that along with companies F, G and H, they were all family businesses. Four out of the thirteen companies detailed in this summary fitted this profile. The researcher also in his investigations identified six other family businesses that fitted this profile, none of whom would agree to be interviewed, preferring to move on and try to forget this ultimate betrayal of trust by a family member.

During a lengthy interview with the owner of company D it became apparent that the MD and owner was blaming himself for not having acted on many early warning signs that he had noticed over a period of some ten years. During the interview he became quite emotional as it became apparent from the line of questions that there had been many early warning signs that he had not recognised. When asked why he had not acted on his suspicions, he said 'Why would I not trust a chartered accountant?' He also remarked that in forty years in business he had never suspected anyone in any of the companies he had worked for of stealing. His suspicions first became apparent when for several months the management accounts indicated significant margin erosion and temporary cash-flow problems. He consulted his accountant regarding his concerns and was told convincingly that there was nothing to worry about and that everything was under control. Unexplained cash-flow problems and margin erosion which is not readily explained are two of the most common corporate early warning signs.

Some ten months after the MD's original suspicions, when to his knowledge things were back to normal, he was asked by the accountant if he could loan the company £150,000. The accountant assured the MD that he only needed the money for a month as the company had a temporary cash-flow problem. Again he was told in a very convincing manner that the temporary position was only due to timing problems with suppliers and hence the request for a short-term loan. The MD agreed and wrote his company a cheque for the amount.

Some three weeks after he made the money available to his company the accountant went away on holiday with his family. After they had been gone for about a week the MD became concerned when one of the accounts staff, a senior bookkeeper of some fifteen years' service, asked the MD what she should do about suppliers pushing for payment. This alarmed the MD. He had a friend who was a chartered accountant and had just retired from a large international company. He asked his friend if he could help him with the accounts on a temporary basis. The friend agreed and came into the office the following day. Within two days the accountant explained to the boss that the company had a very serious cash flow problem. 'How can that be?' the MD asked. 'I loaned the company £150,000 only a month ago.' The accountant then went back to his office and an hour or so later he reported back regarding the loan. The money had in fact been banked but was not treated correctly on the company's accounts. The accountant could find no evidence of the double entry required in accounting.

Some days later it became apparent after the accountant had done more work that £120,000 of the loan had been in his words 'spirited away from the company's books'. By the time the accountant returned to work the size of the fraud was becoming clear. The MD and other directors sat down with the accountant and asked for an explanation of the cash problems; they did not initially refer to their suspicions. After more investigations the MD brought in their auditors. The accountant was suspended pending these investigations. The accountant refused to co-operate with the auditors. He was ultimately dismissed and later diagnosed by a criminal psychologist as suffering from narcissistic personality disorder at severe level.

COMPANY E

This company was an international importer of various materials based in Canada. The company was chosen to investigate as it was the only one that fitted the category in which the owner was also the perpetrator. Many others in this sector were identified, but with this company two directors agreed to take part. The investigation was difficult as interviews and questionnaires had to be carried out by telephone and email after the company had been wound down. There were many products in its portfolio but the main ones were stone, marble, granite, slate etc.

The owner had persuaded several potential directors that he was offering them a wonderful opportunity to help build a new business in Canada and they would eventually reap the rewards. The two directors interviewed invested significant sums of money as shareholders. One took an additional mortgage out on his home and invested $600,000. The other agreed to work for free for the first year and this amount would become his investment, which amounted to about $150,000.

The owner insisted that all the products were paid for by some of his other worldwide subsidiaries. The new directors did not think that this was odd. It was explained as the owner's way of funding this operation. Their mode of operation is wholesale distribution to large DIY stores across North America and Canada. They import from many different countries in the world and the owner has multiple business interest worldwide. He considers himself to be an international entrepreneur.

When the operation had been running for about 18 months, the owner arrived in the office one day and said that he was taking over the administration of the business and particularly the finances. The director who invested the $600,000 was away on vacation. After a few days this director called a board meeting and announced that the FD had been mismanaging the accounts.

The operation was closed down and later it emerged that none of the products had been paid for and there were massive debts to suppliers. All the capital and assets of the company were taken over by the owner for his personal benefit. The directors tried to take legal action for some recovery but their legal advisors discovered that the owner was wanted in the US by the FBI on fraud and mortgage scam felonies.

COMPANY F

The company in question is a private company owned by two partners. One partner is an investor and does not get involved with the day-to-day operations. The company is well established and is in the marble and granite fabrication business, they design and install upmarket products for expensive mansions, as well as hotels and conference centres. The company employs on average 50 to 60 people; some of the staff are only brought in on special contract work. The company employs an outside accountant to prepare the accounts; the day-to-day accounting work is carried out by the office manager/bookkeeper.

Some years ago the office manager, a lady, left the company and was replaced. The owner-manager from time to time used his wife to help out in the business. When the new office manager started she made it very clear that she needed to be left alone to get on with her job and did not require any assistance. After a year or so, the manager asked his wife to help again as the new lady appeared to be working all hours and some weekends. When the wife started to get involved the office manager made it clear that she did not require any assistance and resented the wife's interference. The owner then said to her that as she was working all hours she must require an assistant. She refused, but reluctantly agreed to use the wife on a part-time basis.

The wife became suspicious because the office manager would not let her have access to the company computer system; she changed passwords on a daily basis. The wife was not allowed to do any work associated with the payroll or banking. The wife only tolerated the relationship because the owner thought the office manager was good at her job and trusted her implicitly.

Some six months later the office manager appeared to be very touchy one day. She had arranged to leave early to attend a school function for one of her children, and she had three. The post did not arrive before she left. When the postman did arrive, the wife opened the mail. One of the letters was the latest bank statement with sheets of microfiche copies of company cheques. The wife noticed that there were several cheques which had her husband's signature on them, but she knew the signature in question was not her husband's. She took the paperwork home, but the husband would not accept that his signatures were forged. He spent an hour trying to sign like the signatures on the cheques. Before the wife left the office she tried to find previous bank statements, to no avail. The following day she went to the bank early and obtained copied of bank statements for the previous six months.

The rest is history. The police were called in, the office manager protested her innocence, all to no avail, and was sent to prison. It came out after the court case that this lady had in fact been in jail before, for fraud. The company survived, but only just. The cash flow crisis was managed over time but the company is still finding more of the lady's fiddles. The total she stole from the company was well over one million dollars in an eighteen-month period.

This lady perpetrator had been diagnosed as a psychopath. The wife knew the signs, which is why she distrusted her; her husband did not want to hear her stories as he had been conned. The reason the wife knew the symptoms of a psychopath, was because her father had been one and she had grown up with his compulsive lying and bullying, being manipulative and other traits.

COMPANY G

A 25-year-old produce wholesaling company, this company imports produce from all over the world. The company sells to smaller wholesalers and also many and varied retailers. The owner, the President, started the company from grass roots. Over the years he has employed various family members; in fact his son is now virtually running the day-to-day business. The company is a high margin, very profitable company. Some eight years ago he hired his son-in-law, who eventually became responsible for sales and also purchasing. The owner naturally has been generous with family members; all have company vehicles and exceptional income packages. The son-in-law was paid $150,000 per annum.

About two years ago another family member, a qualified lawyer, noticed that the son-in-law had authorised payment, and indeed initiated payment, to a supplier which had previously been informed in writing that the shipment was faulty and therefore the invoice would not be paid. She researched further and found many anomalies. She asked her father to stay late, and together they found sufficient proof of fraud to challenge the son-in-law. He had stolen in excess of $500,000 directly from the company; he was in collusion with some customers and suppliers to share in fiddles and also had personally borrowed money from other long-standing customers whose owners were personal friends of his father-in-law. He had borrowed the money, telling the owners that he did not have sufficient income from his father-in-law to look after his children properly. The amounts borrowed amounted in total to over $500,000. The son-in-law was confronted by the President and also his wife and her sister, who had discovered the fraud. He confessed and was fired. It later became apparent that he was a gambler and also had a drug addiction, or so he claimed. In exchange for the father-in-law not reporting the theft to the authorities he admitted all of his fiddles and agreed to a divorce. He had in fact also been working weekends, moonlighting for one of his company's competitors. The company did not suffer financially from this fraud. The owner, a wealthy man, saw to this, and he also paid back all the borrowings of his son-in-law.

COMPANY H

This company, a multiple franchise pizzeria with seven restaurants, was a high margin, extremely profitable group. The manager had been put in business by his father-in-law; he had previous experience with

Dominos' Pizza on the sales and marketing side internationally. He was fired under a cloud from this and other positions at senior level; with some companies he was Vice President Marketing. Not all of his history was known at the time he was financed. The father-in-law, is a qualified English accountant. His daughter had met and married her husband, an American citizen, while he was representing Dominos' in the UK. The group manager had a tremendous sense of entitlement, was a compulsive liar and had many psychopathic traits, including violence. He stole company money to buy luxury goods for himself, not always his family; he moved up the home market and ended up financing a million-dollar plus home. The father-in-law discovered the frauds when he could not understand why a high margin business, which was well run had cash flow problems. The son-in-law was fired but the police were not involved. The father-in-law lost most of his invested capital. The only thing to do after he had fired his so-in-law was to sell on the franchises at a loss.

COMPANY I

This company is the UK subsidiary of a European distribution group specialising in selling and maintaining products, mostly add-on hardware for PCs and networking systems. The group at the time of the fraud employed some 260 people. The UK company employed about fifty people split between sales, service personnel and administrative staff and at the time had a turnover of about £14M. This fraud is somewhat different from any of the other companies researched in that the perpetrator was not in the accounts department or in a position in senior management. His fraud required collusion with an outsider. Over a period of some four years this individual had worked himself into a position as a senior salesman specialising in the sale of a product that sold in thousands and had a relatively low unit cost, about three hundred pounds. The company had one major customer who had bought in excess of 10,000 of these units. Many other companies were taking between 50 and 100 units almost every month.

The salesman had from his manager a discount list; this list gave discounts based on the expected number of units sold in a twelve-month period. The salesman was exceedingly successful and each month he achieved his targets, so he was allowed by the sales manager to more or less manage himself. At monthly sales meetings he was nearly always the top achiever, in spite of the fact that his sales manager kept increasing his targets on a three-monthly basis. In a word, this individual was a star.

The managing director of the company was well connected both in business and also the community in which he worked. One morning he took a phone call from the managing director of a systems integration company. He was invited out to lunch the next day, his caller indicated that he had some information that he would like to share. Later the same morning our MD took another call from an ex-employee who had, some ten years previously, started his own business. His company was a user of products bought from the subject firm. He also extended an invitation to lunch.

The MD and his wife, a few weeks before this eventful day, attended a cocktail party. During the course of the evening they were introduced to a member of the local amateur operatic society. During the conversation it became apparent that this operatic lady singer knew a salesman who worked in our MD's company. She remarked that his company must pay their salesmen well, as her singing friend seemed to have an expensive life style. The MD passed over the remark, indicating the man in question was indeed a top salesman.

The MD did not realise that here was a hint that all might not be well. Following the two lunches it became apparent that the salesman had been selling his products to several companies and doing a side deal with the buyers. He had been offering the products at two levels above the call-off rate dictated by the monthly delivery of product. His understanding and agreement was with the purchasing managers in these companies. In short, he was splitting the difference of the unit sale price with the purchasing managers. All three companies therefore had a problem. The salesman was instantly dismissed for dishonesty, as were the buyers in the two companies that had blown the whistle. In the months that followed the sales manager of the supplying company visited all companies who were taking product on a calldown basis. It became apparent that a further six companies had enjoyed the benefits of significantly lower prices. None of them admitted to any wrongdoing.

Estimates as to the value taken were not easy to establish but it was thought that this dishonest salesman had got away with approximately £70,000 during the previous twelve months.

COMPANY J

From being advised about this company it took eighteen months before agreement was finally reached with the victim manager to be interviewed. The company is of particular interest because the information gained helped put into context what had hitherto been suspected but not confirmed, namely the treatment of losses in the company books. This contact was an introduction by a senior executive of a very large international bank. The interviewee was in charge of the commercial mortgage department, and reported to his superior, who was a main board member. He had worked for the bank for almost thirty years at the time of the incident. The reasons for the delay only became evident after the first meeting of four with this victim.

The department was a reasonable size and responsible for hundreds of millions of loans. The department manager had been recruiting for a relatively junior but experienced person to help in the approvals team. A recruit was found, and when he reported for work the manager spent some time with this young man briefing him on the operation. Following this he instructed the new employee to spend the next few weeks reviewing certain files. He was asked to make notes of anything he did not understand and report back. Some days later this new employee asked for a meeting.

The employee had become concerned when he realised that on many of the approval documents there were names and signatures of two people whose names he recognised as having been involved in fraud with his previous job. One was a surveyor and the other a solicitor. It seems that these men had been using an insider in the new recruit's old company to dramatically inflate the valuation of properties and skim money off the top.

After much deliberation and further researching of the files the internal audit team were called in. The bottom line was discovery of fraud amounting to over £8.5 million. The fraudster was summarily dismissed, but the authorities were not informed. This is typical of large organisations; they do not prosecute as they fear bad publicity may harm their business. The researcher agreed to meet his contact in a local coffee bar near to his home. The bank manager had lost his job because the powers that be, and in particular his director boss, had told him that he would have to take the blame for the loss since the fraud was in his department. In their first meeting the interviewee became very distressed and had to abruptly call an end to the meeting. He did agree to meet again, which he did on a further three occasions. He would not agree to a formally recorded interview as he was afraid of repercussions. By meeting on four occasions it turned out to work in favour of the researcher as he was able to make notes immediately following each meeting. (More on this company in Chapter 6, unfair treatments)

COMPANY K

The founder, the Chairman and MD of a company which would not agree to be interviewed two years before, was contacted again recently. His initial refusal was because his perpetrator had left his company with a serious cash-flow problem and he was in the process of trying to save his business. On this occasion he agreed to be interviewed, but only over the telephone. The interview was not recorded but notes were taken during a long telephone conversation. He agreed to describe in as much detail as possible the events leading up to the collapse of his company.

The company was 30 years old and had been profitable for 28 years. Some ten years ago, his son-in-law, a qualified accountant, had approached the founder for a job. The son-in-law had evidently fallen on hard times and lost his position as a senior accountant in a large engineering group. The son-in-law gave a plausible explanation as to the reason for his dismissal. The founder felt that he should give his son-in-law a job to help his daughter and grandchildren, so he hired him as assistant to the finance director. Over the next few years the son-in-law did a great job but had regular conflicts with the finance director, an older man, in his sixties. The FD eventually quit, saying that he wanted to take early retirement. The son-in-law was promoted to FD after the retirement.

The owner had been trying to sell the business for two years prior to the researcher's initial contact. On one occasion he had been offered £7.5m for the company, which he had accepted. A 'heads of agreement' contract had been signed. The buyer pulled out shortly before closing the deal, blaming the son-in-law as the reason. The buyer claimed that he could not trust the son-in-law, to stay with the company long enough for a serious handover. Apparently the son-in-law had made a remark to the accountants who had carried out due diligence that he would be gone in three months.

The owner admitted that with hindsight he should have fired his son-in-law; he did not, because he wanted no hassle in his company and his life. He was semi-retired and really wanted to sell the business.

Just before the researcher's original contact he had been studying the accounts and noticed that there had been, in a particular month, a serious drop in the margins earned. He tackled his son-in-law, who could not, or would not, explain the problem. The old man for some months kept on asking his son-in-law for a satisfactory explanation. None was given. In the end he worked with the sales director, who discovered that all the order processing documents (paper documents) for the particular month showed that the margins had held up and looked normal. This margin drop had apparently cost the company about £50,000 in lost margins and cash flow, which put the company into a loss situation of some £20,000 for the month.

Eventually the company started to have a cash-flow problem and the owner brought in his auditors. They discovered that the son-in-law had been stealing large sums of money from the company over a period of some three years. He had stepped up his take during and after the time when the company was being marketed. The auditors estimated that the total stolen over the three-year period was approximately £650,000, hence the cash-flow problem. The son-in-law was fired and the owner started to try and to raise some money to keep the company afloat. He also put into the company £200,000 from his savings, expecting to be able to save his firm.

When the owner was contacted again after almost two years, he related the final chapter in this sad story of betrayal of trust at its worst. He failed to save his company, the result being that the company assets and goodwill were sold with a pre-pack agreement set up by the administrators. The buyers had agreed to keep on all the staff and also pay the founder for a year as a consultant. They also promised the old man 5% shares in the new company. The only one of these conditions that was kept was to employ all the staff.

When he was asked how he felt now, almost two years since the original contact, the man said he still could not believe that his son-in-law had done this to him. He has had to downsize his home to replace some of the capital he had put into his company in order to be able to live a reasonable life. He blames himself for taking semi-retirement and considers that after many years trying to build the business it should not only have provided for him and his wife, but he should have been able to leave his children some millions when he died.

This businessman had been successful all his working life and because he trusted his son-in-law he now considers himself to be a failed businessman, because he had always intended to sell the company in order to have a comfortable retirement. The entire family, including his son-in-law, knew that this was the plan. The son-in-law moved on and he has no contact with him and little contact with his daughter and grandchildren. He believes that he was taken in by lies and deceit. He had believed the plausible explanation given by his son-in-law when he hired him. During the telephone conversation he kept repeating, 'I trusted him with my money and my retirement'.

This case illustrates the effect occupational fraudsters can have on businessmen who trust them. Why would this man not trust his son-in-law, who was a qualified accountant? To some degree he is still in denial.

During the telephone interview he also repeatedly commented that he still found it all hard to believe, even though his auditors had shown him much proof. He could not bring himself to inform the authorities. He felt that this would be betraying his daughter and grandchildren, not to mention the effect on his other children. This hitherto successful businessman will take his guilt, and to a degree shame, with him to his grave. His feelings of shame come from that fact that his company had to file for administration, the ultimate failure for a businessman. His sin was trust. He trusted his son-in-law and believed a plausible lie.

When questioned about the feelings of his family and his wife he refused to discuss them, with one exception. He explained that his daughter, the one married to the perpetrator, believed that she and her family were the victims. Apparently she believes her husband's lies. The son-in-law told his wife that her father had set him up and was in collusion with the company auditors. When pressed for more on this subject he flatly refused further information, indicating that talking about company events and his feelings was one thing but he would not discuss his family.

This example illustrates how a whole family became victims of a plausible liar and fraudster; he was trusted with not only the finances of the company but also the future of his relatives and the peaceful comfortable retirement of the company founder and his wife. Other victims included some of the staff and their families;

they were fired during the first few months of the new ownership.

ADDITIONAL INVESTIGATIONS

Additional organisations looked at were two large international financial institutions with extensive internal audit facilities and also a large government department. Neither was immune from occupational fraud in spite of extensive anti-fraud policies and internal audit teams. Details of these organisations have been deliberately omitted from this work to ensure confidentiality.

Other companies similar in profile have been omitted from the above descriptions. Several restaurant companies were also initially investigated but were not included in the main research, as the losses were not sufficiently high in monetary terms to justify inclusion in this research. In total over 50 companies were initially investigated, with only 21 given the full interview and questionnaire treatment.

CHAPTER FOUR

Personality Disorders

HISTORIC DEFINITIONS - PYSCHOPATHY

In looking at the incidence of pyschopathy in companies who have become victims of occupational fraud, it is important to first understand just what is being investigated. Three terms need to be defined: pyschopathy, white-collar crime and occupational fraud.

What exactly is meant by the term 'pyschopathy'? In basic terms it is used to explain and define personality disorders. Sam Vaknin, in his article on the history of personality disorders, discusses the beginnings of literature on the subject (Vaknin 2006). He states:

'Well into the eighteenth century, the only types of mental illness - then collectively known as 'delirium' or 'mania' - were depression (melancholy), psychoses, and delusions. At the beginning of the nineteenth century, the French psychiatrist Pinel coined the phrase 'manie sans delire' (insanity without delusions). He described patients who lacked impulse control, often raged when frustrated, and were prone to outbursts of violence. He noted that such patients were not subject to delusions. He was referring, of course, to psychopaths (subjects with antisocial personality disorder).

Across the ocean in the United States, Benjamin Rush made similar observations. In 1835 J C Pritchard, working as Senior Physician at the Bristol Infirmary (hospital), published a seminal work titled *Treatise on Insanity and Other Disorders of the Mind*. He in turn suggested the neologism 'moral insanity'. To quote him, moral insanity consisted of 'a morbid perversion of the natural feelings, affections, inclinations, temper, habits, moral dispositions, and natural impulses without any remarkable disorder or defect of the intellect or knowing or reasoning faculties and in particular without any insane delusion or hallucination' (Vaknin 2006).

Further research into the history of pyschopathy and the history of personality disorders indicates that a German psychiatrist, Julius Ludwig August Koch, published a short textbook of psychiatry in 1888. In this book he mentioned the term 'psychopathic inferiority'. His following work *Die Psychopathischen Minderwertigkeiten* (1891-1893), became one of the fundamental textbooks concerning the concept of disorders of personality. These concepts are still in use today. In his book, published in three parts, he tried to describe the whole field of psychic normality and psychoses. Although psychiatric disorders are classified differently today, Koch's work is still important in the field of personality disorders. Furthermore one can find exact and detailed descriptions of many psychopathological symptoms still worth reading one hundred and twenty years later (Wurzbg Medizinhist, 2006.)

Schneider superseded Koch's work in 1923. Schneider, in his work *Psychopathic Personalities*, established psychopathy as a subclass of abnormal personality and suggested ten different forms of the psychopathic syndrome. In 1939 Henderson, in his work *Psychopathic States*, set the pattern that was to characterise Anglo-American delineations of the disorder. Henderson concentrated on the most severe forms of psychopathic abnormalities, concentrating on the anti-social nature of the condition (Vaknin 2006). Later, in 1941, Cleckley in his book *The Mask of Sanity* further narrowed the category to aggressive psychopaths and established criteria for the disorder centred round anti-social behaviour. Cleckley states: 'Beauty and ugliness, except in a very superficial sense, goodness, evil, love, horror and humour, have no actual meaning, no power to move him' (Cleckley 1941).

Following Cleckley, in 1950 and in 1959, another German psychiatrist, K Schneider, published two books: *The Psychopathic Personality 9th Edition* (1950) and *Clinical Psychopathology* (1959). In these works Schneider expanded the diagnosis to include people who harm and inconvenience themselves as well as others.

Patients who were depressed, socially anxious, excessively shy and insecure were all deemed by

Schneider to be 'psychopaths' or abnormal. Many others made contributions culminating in the definitions contained in *ICD-10 Classifications of Mental and Behavioural Disorders* (European Standards, 1992) and *DSM-1V Diagnosis and Statistical Manual of Mental Disorders* (The American Psychiatric Association, 1994). These two publications claim to be compatible and are used extensively today for defining and diagnosing mental and personality disorders worldwide.

Ten personality disorders are listed in DSM-IV R. These are split into three groups. The first group are the **Eccentric Personality Disorders**. These people often appear strange or peculiar to others. They are classed as follows:

Paranoid Personality Disorder: Individual generally tends to interpret the actions of others as threatening.

Schizoid Personality Disorder: This individual is generally detached from social relationships, and shows a narrow range of emotional expression in various social settings.

Schizotypal Personality Disorder: People with this disorder are uncomfortable in close relationships, have thought or perceptual distortions, and peculiarities of behaviour.

The second group are the **Dramatic Personality Disorders**. These people have intense emotional mood swings and distorted perceptions of themselves and impulsive behaviours:

The person with **Anti-Social Personality Disorder** shows a disregard for others and violates their rights. Often exhibits criminal tendencies.

The **Borderline Personality Disorder** individual shows a generalized pattern of instability in interpersonal relationship, self-image, and observable emotions and significant impulsiveness.

The person with **Histrionic Personality Disorder** often displays excessive emotionality and attention-seeking characteristics. HPDs tend to overreact to other people, and can be perceived as shallow and self-centred.

The **Narcissistic Personality Disorder** individual has a grandiose view of him/herself, a need for admiration and a lack of empathy. The condition begins by early adulthood and is present in various situations. These individuals are very demanding in their relationships.

Two disorders out of this group, Narcissistic Personality Disorder and Anti-Social Personality Disorder, along with the Psychopath (Sociopath), have been associated with white-collar crime (occupational fraud).

The third group are the **Anxious Personality Disorders**. These people are often fearful and anxious.

Avoidant Personality Disorder: Socially inhibited, feels inadequate, and is sensitive to criticism.

Dependent Personality Disorder: An extreme need to be taken care of that leads to fears of separation and passive and clinging behaviour.

Obsessive-Compulsive Personality Disorder: Preoccupied with orderliness, perfectionism and control at the expense of flexibility, openness, and efficiency.

DISORDERS AND FRAUD

For decades accountants have listed elements that need to be present for occupational fraud to take place. One such definition:

1) An economic or psychological need
2) A moral justification, sense of entitlement
3) An opportunity
4) A perceived low chance of detection (Comer 1977)

A psychological need and a sense of entitlement would tend to point the way to personality disorders in perpetrators. Some of the perpetrators of the large corporations mentioned may fit into this category. As an example, Andy Fastow, the creative accountant in Enron, certainly felt that he had entitlement. Fastow is now serving a reduced sentence of 10 years for occupational fraud. His sentence was reduced for helping the authorities by agreeing to testify against other Enron executives. He also paid back $23M. (The

Enron trials 2002-2006) Fastow was a classic case of looking after number one. When caught, he let his wife Lea take a rap for her part in his fraudulent schemes, and she went to jail for a year.

Three defined personality disorders are the NPD (Narcissistic Personality Disorder), ASPD (Anti-Social Personality Disorder) and the Psychopath or Sociopath. Psychopaths, have been diagnosed in many cases of occupational fraud. These personality defects share some common traits and indeed the term 'narcissistic psychopath' is used in some papers on the subject. Sam Vaknin, himself an NPD, is the author of *Malignant Self Love-Narcissism Revisited* (Vaknin 2006). Vaknin was diagnosed as an NPD whilst serving time in an Israeli jail after being convicted on fraud-related chargers. In an interview for Radio National Australia on the subject of 'psychopaths in suits' he stated: 'Many narcissists are also psychopaths and most psychopaths also have narcissistic traits, or a narcissistic style, or even a narcissistic personality, so the distinctions are blurred, and many people think that they are artificial. There's very rarely a pure diagnosis of narcissism'.

Comparing the definitions of personality traits of both NPDs and psychopaths listed below, it is easy to understand Vaknin's comment that the distinctions are blurred. Some of the text below on NPD is taken direct from DSM-1V. Although ICD-10 definitions are essentially the same, most researchers and academics seem to always refer to the American manual.

NARCISSISTIC PERSONALITY DISORDER

Most people will have heard the term narcissist, referring to the Greek god or indeed the daffodil-like flower the narcissus. The narcissus blooms early in the spring and is often found in damp soil near to a pond. It is a self-sufficient, fertile but stagnant environment. The flower is usually of six white vesica-shaped radiating petals with a central yellow funnel containing the stamen and the stigma. The stem bends just before the blossom, tilting it so the blossom faces out or down rather than up. According to myth, this is because Narcissus was gazing down at his reflection when he was transformed into the flower. The stalk is otherwise firm and upright. In Islam the Hadith of Bukhari associates the flower with the upright and righteous man. The symbol has also been likened to the transformation of vanity and self-centredness into the humility of a more individuated and spiritual self.

The name 'Narcissus' derives from the Greek word 'narke', meaning numb, from which we also get the word 'narcotic'. The Greek's narcissism stood for vanity, callousness and insensitivity. Narcissus was emotionally numb to those who fell in love with him and with his beauty.

Greek mythology is not clear as to the parentage of Narcissus. He was loved by Apollo and counted as one of the most handsome of young men. Some say he was the son of the river God Cephisus and the Nymph

Liriope, while others have him being the son of Endymion and Selene. The beauty of Narcissus could be compared to Adonis, whom Aphrodite loved, or to Endymion, whom Selene loved, and various other mythological couples.

Simplistically, the beautiful Narcissus discovered his image in a pond or the river and fell in love with the image. Supposedly he died of sorrow by the pool. It is said that Narcissus still keeps gazing on his image in the waters of the river Styx in the underworld.

There are at least two different accounts with regard to the legend of Narcissus. Ovid's version and Archaic's version seem to be the most popular.

Ovid's version:

Ovid tells the story of a pretty and graceful nymph named Echo who loved Narcissus in vain. Narcissus himself felt that his beauty was so unmatched and godlike that he compared himself to the beauty of Bacchus and Apollo. As a direct result of this belief, Narcissus spurned Echo's affections until she faded away to nothing but a plaintive whisper. To teach Narcissus a lesson, the goddess Nemesis condemned him to fall in love with his own reflection in Echo's pond. Narcissus, enamoured by his own beauty and image, lay on the riverbank and wasted away while staring at the water.

A slightly different version of the story tells how Narcissus, after scorning his male suitors, was cursed by the gods to love the first male he should lay his eyes on. While walking in the gardens of Echo, Narcissus discovered the pond of Echo. He saw his own reflection in the pond, fell deeply in love with himself and as he leaned closer to the beautiful reflection he fell into the pond and drowned.

Archaic version:

This version is a more moral tale than the Ovid version. In this one Narcissus, being proud and uncaring, is punished by the gods for having spurned his male suitors. It is thought to have been a cautionary tale addressed to adolescent boys.

The source of this version was from a segment in Pausanias about 150 years after the Ovid Version. A similar account was discovered in the Oxyrhynchus papyri in 2004. This account predates the Ovid version by about 50 years. The ending is different in that Narcissus, not realising that it was his own reflection that he was looking at, took his sword and killed himself from sorrow. The nymphs mourned for him, including Echo. They prepared a funeral pile and would have burned the body, but it was nowhere to be found. They found a flower in the place where Narcissus had died. The flower was purple inside and was surrounded with white leaves; this flower bears the name Narcissus and preserves the memory (nationmaster.com 2011).

The diagnostic and statistical manual of mental disorders covers ten personality disorders and defines Narcissistic Personality Disorder (NPD) as follows:

A pervasive pattern of grandiosity (in fantasy or behaviour), a need for admiration and lack of empathy, beginning by early adulthood and present in a variety of contexts, as indicated by five (or more) of the following:

(1) has a grandiose sense of self-importance (eg exaggerates achievements and talents, expects to be recognized as superior without commensurate achievements).

(2) is preoccupied with fantasies of unlimited success, power, brilliance, beauty, or ideal love.

(3) believes that he or she is 'special' and unique and can only be understood by, or should associate with, other special or high-status people (or institutions).

(4) requires excessive admiration.

(5) has a sense of entitlement, ie unreasonable expectations of especially favourable treatment or automatic compliance with his or her expectations.

(6) is interpersonally exploitative, ie takes advantage of others to achieve his or her own ends.

7) lacks empathy: is unwilling to recognize or identify with the feelings and needs of others.

(8) is often envious of others or believes that others are envious of him or her.

(9) shows arrogant, haughty behaviours or attitudes. (DSM-1V)

Expanding these brief definitions into plain English, it becomes easier to understand the diverse and somewhat abnormal behaviour characteristics of people who suffer from such disorders. Perhaps it is incorrect to refer to such human beings as 'suffering'. In many cases, in particular the ones who exhibit all nine characteristics, they do not suffer in the same way as many humans who have clinical mental illness conditions.

An exaggerated sense of self-importance leads the subject to exaggerate achievements and talents and expect to be recognized as superior without achievements to back it up. Grandiosity is the hallmark of narcissism. People with NPD portray grandiosity to the extreme. Normal people see it as extreme arrogance. The simplest everyday way in which narcissists show their exaggerated sense of self-importance is by talking about family, work, and life in general as if there is nobody else in the picture. Whatever they may be doing, in their own view, they are the star, and they give the impression that they are bearing heroic responsibility for their family or department or company, that they have to take care of everything because their spouses or co-workers are undependable, uncooperative, or otherwise unfit. They ignore the abilities and contributions of others in business and often complain that they receive no help.

They tend to be preoccupied with fantasies, success, power and brilliance; for example in the author's research one such narcissist was often heard over many years commenting 'when I am rich and famous'. Rich he became with his ill-gotten games, but not famous. He has probably now moved on from his fraudulent behaviour and in narcissistic terms still fantasises about the future.

Other narcissists' fantasies manifest in them living in their own world of make-believe. To the outside world they portray the person or persons they would be by acting accordingly. When challenged and reality intrudes into their world they may react with indignation and anger.

The narcissist strongly believes that he/she is 'special' and can only associate with other special or high-status people, assuming such individuals to be of use to them. Narcissists think that everyone who is not special and superior is worthless. By definition, normal or average people are not superior, as they are, and are no use to them.

Narcissists require excessive admiration in more than one way; they are always seeking praise, compliments and suggestions of envy and indeed they themselves can also envy others. They want to be told that everything they do is superior to their perception of others. They always seem to believe that others are envious of them, in other words they are not trying to 'keep up with the Joneses' - they are the Joneses.

Narcissists have a strong sense of entitlement. They expect automatic compliance with their wishes; they always expect to be treated favourably. For example in a queue situation they expect to be allowed to go first. Narcissists quite often react with anger or rage when these unreasonable expectations and desires are not met, defined as a narcissistic rage.

Narcissists takes advantage of others in a dramatic way, exploiting and manipulating them in business for personal gain. They are always using colleagues and friends to achieve what they want. They do not care about the cost to their victims, as they have no empathy with others. They can even destroy individuals and cause them to have breakdowns or worse (discussed more fully in chapter 5, Betrayal of Trust).

Narcissists are totally lacking in empathy. They are unwilling to recognize or sympathize with other people's feelings and needs and 'switch off' when other people want to talk about their problems. In clinical terms, empathy is an ability to recognize and interpret other people's emotions and feelings.

Narcissists display arrogant behaviour and can be very patronising. They are contemptuous of others and look down on human beings that they believe to be less intelligent than they see themselves to be. They ditch people they have used when they see no further advantage to them and treat people, family friends and colleagues like dirt.

In summary, the NPD is arrogant, requires admiration, is envious of others and is interpersonally exploitive. He/she shows a lack of empathy towards other human

Psychologists using recommendations in DSM-1V diagnose NPD when five or more of the above traits are observed. Certainly when a subject displays all nine characteristic traits there would be no doubt. However to display all the NPD traits would also mean that the subject would score high in the Hare PCL-R checklist (Psychopathy Checklist Revised, see below) for psychopathy, indicating a psychopath or sociopath diagnosis.

Three levels of NPD are defined:

Mild:

When egotistical behaviour results in occasional minor problems, but the person is generally doing pretty well in their chosen profession and integrates reasonably well into society.

Moderate:

a) Missing days from work.

b) Significant performance problems as a wage-earner, homemaker, or student.

c) Frequently avoiding or alienating friends.

d) Significant risk of harming self or others (maybe some suicidal preoccupation).

e) Often neglecting family.

f) Frequently abusing others.

g) Committing criminal acts.

Severe:

a)   Staying in bed all day.

b)   Totally alienating all friends and family.

c)   Severe risk of harming self or others.

d)   Failing to maintain personal hygiene.

e)   Danger of suicide.

f)   Abuse of others.

g)   Criminal activities (DSM-1V).

NPDs never accept responsibility for any problems their behaviour may have caused and they will tend to blame others for their extreme actions. Their egotistical behaviour is not per se caused by drug or alcohol abuse, nor is it because of a psychiatric state or condition. Industrial psychologists believe the extreme behaviour of NPDs may develop in adolescence. NPDs in business quite often verbally abuse colleagues, which impairs their functional ability in their occupations. NPDs quite often contradict themselves, sometimes within the same sentence.

How does the NPD condition start? Is it nature, ie genetic, or could it be nurture? The psychologists say that theories regarding the development of NPD revolve around issues of unmet basic childhood needs. Narcissistic defences in babies are innately present during the first eighteen months of an infant's life. The infant experiences being the centre of his mother's world, which makes the child feel powerful in a basic sense. A child's world has no limits.

One theory suggests that near the end of the first eighteen months of a child's life a psychological transformation causes the disintegration or separation of the child's oneness with the mother. During this separation period, if the mother is not responsive and sensitive to the child's needs then NPD can develop.

Other theories put forward by psychologists suggest that the development of a child's ego is governed by the limits put on it and the consequences of these limits that the parents set during the first two to ten years. -

To be diagnosed as an NPD as stated above, the accepted criteria is when five or more of the traits are exhibited in a person. With NPDs in the severe category, if they take to crime it seems to be more often than not associated with money and fraud. Because of their grandiosity and belief that they are smarter than all others, they really believe that they can never be caught. This makes the condition difficult if not impossible to treat.

Psychologists believe NPD behaviour characteristics begin to develop in the teens and early adulthood. An NPD is unable to trust others but relies on others to be a mirror which reflects back to him his accomplishments and talents, however unrealistic these beliefs may be. This is referred to in psychology as a 'narcissistic Supply'.

In basic terms a narcissistic person has an extremely fragile sense of self-worth. Deep down the NPD feels inferior. He depends on and needs the admiration and attention of others in order to strengthen his negative feelings of self-worth and inferiority. Whilst he is envious of others, he also believes others are envious of him, particularly relative to his possessions. He is constantly seeking compliments and admiration.

The NPD may tend to develop shallow associations and relationships with people he portrays as friends. These so-called friends he uses to extract compliments to help satisfy his needs. A narcissistic person can display a rapid change in attitudes and morality. He is always ready to shift values to gain favour. Because of this trait any normal interaction with a narcissist is difficult at best, but in most cases impossible.

Narcissists are very self-centred and self-absorbing and have no interest in anyone other than themselves. The narcissistic mode of operation is to form friendships or romantic associations with individuals who can enhance their self-esteem. These relationships are often cultivated solely to enhance the NPD's career.

Listening to an NPD talk, you would never realise his or her true lack of self-esteem. A narcissist always presents a false image to the world. Beneath this inferiority there is a preoccupation with fantasy, ideal love and unreal achievement and a tendency towards superficial interests usually picked up from others, hence the superficiality. The narcissist will often uses others to help him with any project or task that he undertakes. He will then take credit for the outcome of work which others have done.

The narcissistic individual can be, and often is, successful at his chosen career. This is because his workplace and environment provides him with a narcissistic supply. An NPD's awareness and recognition is impaired to the extent that he frequently misinterprets others' words, actions and thoughts. He may believe that someone respects or loves him, yet this is a fantasy which exists only in his own mind. Narcissists exaggerate their own accomplishments and are boastful and pretentious. They frequently compare themselves to people who have accomplished a great deal and are surprised when others do not agree.

A narcissist will often try to impress others with his knowledge and decisiveness, yet a narcissistic person's knowledge is often trivial. His ideas are almost never original. He chooses to quote whoever he feels at the time is an authority; however, the quotations may not be what the chosen authority actually said. The narcissist makes his own interpretations to suit his purpose at the time. He also feels that only people of high status can understand him, and he often assigns special, gifted, or unique qualities to the people with whom he associates. He will insist that he has the best doctor, lawyer, accountant, bank manager etc. available, and will assign nonfactual accomplishments to that individual to prove the validity of his claims.

A narcissistic individual displays beliefs and behaviours that indicate a sense of being special. He expects favourable treatment from others and demands immediate compliance with his requests. For instance he does not feel he should be made to queue, and expects to be the centre of attention. He is mystified when he does not get what he wants. If an individual disappoints him, he will devalue that person to others. A narcissist demonstrates a lack of empathy towards others and this causes him to treat others like dirt. He does not see others as human beings, but sees them as objects that have no feelings or needs. His sense of entitlement leads to his exploitation of others and these exploitations results in very little guilt or remorse. An NPD's children can often be seen in his eyes as possessions and not human beings.

A 'narcissistic injury' occurs when someone criticises the narcissistic person. The narcissist may not show it outwardly, but he is haunted by criticisms and defeats. He does have emotions. The narcissist, however, does not relate to his emotions as others do because he represses them so deeply that they play no conscious role in his behaviour. In fact, these repressed emotions unconsciously play a large part in determining his behaviour. When a narcissistic injury occurs, the subject begins to feel empty, degraded, and humiliated and may retaliate with narcissistic rage. This rage can manifest itself in actual physical abuse, but is more likely to be verbal, albeit extreme, depending on the level and which category the individual comes under, eg mild, moderate or severe.

A classic example of narcissistic rage is the case of

Brian Blackwell from Liverpool. Brian was a straight A student who played a reasonable game of tennis and created an image of an up-and-coming tennis star. His lies included claiming to have an endorsement worth £70,000 a year from Nike. He hired his girlfriend as his secretary and gave her a cheque for £40,000 taken from his parents' bank. His claims were challenged by his parents, provoking a narcissistic rage. This led him to murder his parents by bludgeoning them to death with a clawhammer. He then took his girlfriend on an expensive holiday using their credit cards. This case is a classic example of an NPD at severe level (Channel 4 TV 2005).

The charge of murder was reduced to manslaughter after court-appointed psychiatrists and psychologists testified that as Blackwell was in a narcissistic rage at the time, the crime was clearly not premeditated (Channel 4 2005). Whilst accepting this diagnosis as fair and accurate, this diagnosis of Blackwell as NPD at severe level would almost automatically mean that he would score high in the Hare PCL-R (see below). Could Blackwell therefore have been an NPD with psychopathic ways, or indeed a narcissistic psychopath?

A typical NPD, when challenged, flies into a narcissistic rage and becomes a different person from the image normally portrayed. He can often when in such a rage have an evil and predatory look in his eyes. In extreme cases, as in Blackwell, the result can be violence and murder. In less aggressive NPDs verbal bullying takes place, which in some of the cases described to the author results in grown adults, both men and women, bursting into tears. In one company interviewed by the author there were several examples of male senior managers succumbing to this abuse. In the same company one employee died from a heart attack following a severe dressing down by an NPD earlier that day, despite having no previous history of heart problems. There is no proof that his death was caused by the verbal abuse he had endured, but it certainly caused extreme stress which could have aggravated a dormant and undiagnosed heart condition.

IDENTIFYING AND DIAGNOSING NARCISSISTIC PERSONALITY DISORDER

Narcissistic disturbance can be found in everyone. An individual's existence would be in jeopardy if some narcissistic traits were not present. These traits protect the ego from severe damage inflicted by others, thus keeping our self-esteem intact. NPD occurs when narcissistic traits and behaviour become exaggerated.

Anti-Social Personality Disorder (ASPD) is a psychiatric condition characterized by an individual's common disregard for social rules, norms, and cultural codes, as well as impulsive behaviour and indifference to the rights and feelings of others. The terms is used by the American Psychiatric Association's Diagnostic and Statistical Manual, while the World Health Organization's ICD-10 refers to Dissocial Personality Disorder.

The manual lists the following additional necessary criteria:

1 Failure to conform to social norms with respect to lawful behaviours, as indicated by repeatedly performing acts which are grounds for arrest.

2. Deceitfulness, as indicated by repeated lying, use of aliases, or conning others or personal profit or pleasure.

3. Impulsivity or failure to plan ahead.

4. Irritability and aggressiveness, as indicated by repeated physical fights or Assaults.

5. Reckless disregard for safety of self or others.

6. Consistent irresponsibility, as indicated by repeated failure to sustain steady work or honour financial obligations.

7. Lack of remorse, as indicated by being indifferent to or rationalizing having hurt, mistreated, or stolen from another.

The manual lists the following additional necessary criteria:

- The individual is at least 18 years of age.
- There is evidence of conduct disorder with onset before age 15 years.
- The occurrence of antisocial behaviour is not exclusively during the course of schizophrenia or a manic episode (DSM-1V-TR).

THE PSYCHOPATH

The Hare psychopathy check list PCL-R is a tool designed by Professor Robert Hare and used worldwide to assess psychopaths. It is an expansion of the Cleckley characteristic traits. In his book *The Mask of Sanity*, first published in 1941, Cleckley first details the sixteen traits originally outlined by Kahn. In his work, which is primarily concerned with psychopathology in general, Kahn, in accordance with established practice, lists types which have been almost universally quoted as characteristic subdivisions into which the psychopath can be classified:

1. The nervous
2. The anxious
3. The sensitive
4. The compulsive
5. The excitable
6. The hyperthymic
7. The depressive
9. The affectively cold
10. The weak-willed
11. The impulsive
12. The sexually perverse
13. The hysterical
14. The fantastic

15. The cranks

16. The eccentric

(Cleckley, The Mask Of Sanity, 5th edition: P234)

Cleckley develops from the above his own sixteen characteristic traits of the psychopath. These primary traits were then developed by Hare into PCL-R:

'Before going on to the perhaps still unanswerable questions of why the psychopath behaves as he does or how he comes to follow such a life scheme, let us, as was just suggested, attempt to say what the psychopath is in terms of his actions and his apparent intentions, so that we may recognize him readily and distinguish him from others. We shall list the characteristic points that have emerged and then discuss them in order:

1. Superficial charm and good 'intelligence'
2. Absence of delusions and other signs of irrational thinking
3. Absence of 'nervousness' or psychoneurotic manifestations
4. Unreliability
5. Untruthfulness and insincerity
6. Lack of remorse or shame
7. Inadequately motivated antisocial behaviour
8. Poor judgment and failure to learn by experience

9. Pathologic egocentricity and incapacity for love

10. General poverty in major affective reactions

11. Specific loss of insight

12. Unresponsiveness in general interpersonal relations

13. Fantastic and uninviting behaviour with drink and sometimes without

14. Suicide rarely carried out

15. Sex life impersonal, trivial and poorly integrated

16. Failure to follow any life plan

(Cleckley, The Mask Of Sanity, 5th edition: P339)

Below is the Hare PCL-R:

1. GLIB and SUPERFICIAL CHARM - the tendency to be smooth, engaging, charming, slick and verbally facile. A person with psychopathic charm is not in the least shy, self-conscious, or afraid to say anything. A psychopath never gets tongue-tied. They have freed themselves from the social conventions about taking turns in talking, for example.

2. GRANDIOSE SELF-WORTH - a grossly inflated view of one's abilities and self-worth, self-assured, opinionated, cocky, a braggart. Psychopaths are arrogant people who believe they are superior human beings.

3. NEED FOR STIMULATION or PRONENESS TO BOREDOM - an excessive need for novel, thrilling and exciting stimulation; taking chances and doing things that are risky. Psychopaths often have a low self-discipline in carrying tasks through to completion because they get bored easily. They fail to work at the same job for any length of time, for example, or to finish tasks that they consider dull or routine.

4. PATHOLOGICAL LYING - can be moderate or high; in moderate form, they will be shrewd, crafty, cunning, sly, and clever; in extreme form, they will be deceptive, deceitful, underhanded, unscrupulous, manipulative, and dishonest.

5. CONNING AND MANIPULATIVENESS - the use of deceit and deception to cheat, con, or defraud others for personal gain; distinguished from Item #4 in the degree to which exploitation and callous ruthlessness is present, as reflected in a lack of concern for the feelings and suffering of one's victims.

6. LACK OF REMORSE OR GUILT - a lack of feelings or concern for the losses, pain and suffering of victims; a tendency to be unconcerned, dispassionate, cold hearted and unempathetic. This item is usually demonstrated by a disdain for one's victims.

7. SHALLOW AFFECT - emotional poverty or a limited range or depth of feelings; interpersonal coldness in spite of signs of open gregariousness.

8. CALLOUSNESS and LACK OF EMPATHY - a lack of feelings towards people in general; cold, contemptuous, inconsiderate and tactless.

9. PARASITIC LIFESTYLE - an intentional, manipulative, selfish and exploitative financial dependence on others as reflected in a lack of motivation, low self-discipline and inability to begin or complete responsibilities.

10. POOR BEHAVIOURAL CONTROLS - expressions of irritability, annoyance, impatience, threats, aggression and verbal abuse; inadequate control of anger and temper; acting hastily.

11. PROMISCUOUS SEXUAL BEHAVIOUR - a variety of brief, superficial relations, numerous affairs and an indiscriminate selection of sexual partners; the maintenance of several relationships at the same time; a history of attempts to sexually coerce others into sexual activity or taking great pride at discussing sexual exploits or conquests.

12. EARLY BEHAVIOUR PROBLEMS - a variety of behaviours prior to age 13, including lying, theft, cheating, vandalism, bullying, sexual activity, fire-setting, glue-sniffing, alcohol use, and running away from home.

13. LACK OF REALISTIC, LONG-TERM GOALS - an inability or persistent failure to develop and execute long-term plans and goals; a nomadic existence, aimless, lacking direction in life.

14. IMPULSIVITY - the occurrence of behaviours that are unpremeditated and lack reflection or planning; inability to resist temptation, frustrations, and urges; a lack of deliberation without considering the consequences; foolhardy, rash, unpredictable, erratic, and reckless.

15. IRRESPONSIBILITY - repeated failure to fulfil or honor obligations and commitments, such as not paying bills, defaulting on loans, performing sloppy work, being absent or late to work, failing to honour contractual agreements.

16. FAILURE TO ACCEPT RESPONSIBILITY FOR OWN ACTIONS - a failure to accept responsibility for one's actions, reflected in low conscientiousness, an absence of dutifulness, antagonistic manipulation, denial of responsibility, and an effort to manipulate others through this denial.

17. MANY SHORT-TERM MARITAL RELATIONSHIPS - a lack of commitment to a long-term relationship, reflected in inconsistent, undependable and unreliable commitments in life, including marital.

18. JUVENILE DELINQUENCY - behaviour problems between the ages of 13-18; mostly behaviours that are crimes or clearly involve aspects of antagonism, exploitation, aggression, manipulation, or a callous, ruthless tough-mindedness.

19. REVOCATION OF CONDITION RELEASE - a revocation of probation or other conditional release due to technical violations, such as carelessness, low deliberation, or failing to appear.

20. CRIMINAL VERSATILITY - a diversity of types of criminal offences, regardless of whether the person has been arrested or convicted for them; taking great pride at getting away with crimes.

The Hare PCL-SV (Screening version)

A screening version of this test, the Hare PCL-SV (psychology check list, screening version) is shown below. This test used by psychologists for screening has a maximum score of 24 as opposed to the full PCL-R, which has a maximum of 40. In PCL-R some use a cut-off score of 30, whereas others use 25 for a diagnosis of a psychopath. Scoring is to mark 2 for the characteristic trait being always present and 1 for the trait being present some of the time with a 0 score for never present.

Interpersonal Lifestyle
Superficial
Impulsive

Grandiose

Lacks goals

Deceitful

Irresponsible

Affective

Anti-Social

Lacks Remorse

Poor Behavioural control

Lacks Empathy

Adolescent anti-social behaviour

Does not accept responsibility

Adult anti-social behaviour

The psychopath, a word defining certain personality traits, has been studied for at least a hundred years. On the other hand Narcissistic Personality Disorder was defined only in the 1980s. It is not surprising therefore that there is much more information on psychopaths and more studies than there are relative to NPDs.

Hare's book *Without Conscience* would seem to be applicable in describing both psychopaths and people suffering from Narcissistic Personality Disorder. Hare however does not refer to NPDs in his book.

To more fully understand the similarities of NPDs and Psychopaths, refer to tables in the appendices. Appendix 2 is the full excerpt from DSM-1V on the Hare PCL-R.

The author's research did not attempt to categorise or diagnose perpetrators; the plan was, in general terms, to identify the incidence of psychopathy in cases of occupational fraud by finding out if managers and colleagues of perpetrators have witnessed characteristic traits as in the tables shown. This approach was intended to indicate the presence of psychopathy from observed behavioural characteristic traits, regardless of a professional diagnosis.

The Hare Psychopathy Checklist Revised (PCL-R) is a diagnostic tool used to rate a person's psychopathic and antisocial tendencies. Individuals who are psychopathic prey ruthlessly on others using charm, deceit, violence or other methods that allow them to get what they want. The symptoms of psychopathy include lack of a conscience or sense of guilt, lack of empathy, egocentricity, pathological lying, repeated violations of social norms, disregard for the law, shallow emotions and a history of victimizing others.

The PCL-R is used for diagnosing psychopathy in individuals for clinical, legal or research purposes. Developed in the early 1990s, the test was originally designed to identify the level of a person's psychopathic tendencies. Because psychopaths are often repeat offenders who commit sexual assaults or other violent crimes repeatedly, PCL-R testing is now finding use in the courtroom and in institutions as an indicator of the potential risk posed by subjects or prisoners. In some countries the results of the tests have been used in forensic courtroom settings as a factor in deciding the length and type of prison sentences and if treatment subjects should be tried.

Obviously, diagnosing someone as a psychopath is a very serious step. It has important implications for a person and for his or her associates in family, clinical and forensic settings. Therefore, the test must be administered by professionals who have been specifically trained in its use and who have a wide-ranging and up-to-date familiarity with studies of psychopathy.

Professionals who administer the diagnostic examination should have advanced degrees (MD, PhD or DEd) in a medical, behavioural or social science field and be registered with a reputable organization which oversees psychiatric or psychological testing and diagnostic procedures. Other recommendations include experience working with convicted or accused criminals, or several years of some other related on-the-job training. Because the results are used so often in legal cases, those who administer it should be qualified to serve as expert witnesses in the courtroom. It is also a good idea, if possible, for two experts to test a subject independently with the PCL-R. The final rating would then be determined by averaging their scores.

Many studies conducted in North America and Europe attest to the value of the PCLR for evaluating an individual's psychopathic characteristic traits. In some countries these tests are used for predicting the likelihood of future violent behaviour.

In this vein, during 1999, the British Government released a consultation document that had many psychiatrists and indeed civil rights campaigners protesting. The document title was 'Managing Dangerous People with Severe Personality Disorders'. This document proposed that such people could be detained using mental health law on the grounds of public protection, whether or not they had committed a crime (HMSO 1999).

Many psychiatrists and psychologists have been extremely critical of the concept of incarcerating individuals based on the Hare PCL-R. It is one thing using tests to establish if a criminal has psychopathic tendencies before sentencing, but the idea of locking up individuals who had not committed a criminal act based on such a tool seems to many to be not only morally wrong and an affront to the individual's human rights but an extremely flawed concept. There is much written on this subject. One such paper by Dr Bob Johnson, 'An analysis of medical and legal flaws in PCL-R', covers this controversial subject very well and outlines many of the concerns by others. The following extracts from this paper serve to illustrate many of the objections. Dr Johnson states in his opening paragraph:

'It is perhaps the most widespread of such tests, and is used throughout the world. It is frequently used in the UK often just before a prisoner or long-term mental patient is about to be released. Any score above 28 in Texas reputedly incurs the death penalty. The bulk of the items scored are historic and cannot change — so to use this test as a predictor of future behaviour rules out the possibility of change, or of emotional maturation, let alone of 'burn out'. Despite its apparently straightforward nature, the test has serious flaws — flaws which are not necessarily apparent to those who know only one side of the story, but which become much clearer if viewed with soundly based common sense'.

Johnson goes on to discuss legal intent and risk assessment as well as quoting some of Hare's own concerns:

'A question of intent: The use of the Hare Psychopathy Check List (Revised) (PCL-R) in the criminal justice system sometimes leads to the conclusion that it is primarily a risk instrument rather than what it really is, a measure of a psychological construct.' (emphasis added)

Professor Hare here highlights the fundamental flaw which leads to his test being widely misapplied, if not actually abused — with dire consequences, not only for those 'tested': 'Professor Hare correctly distinguishes between risk assessment on the one hand, and 'a psychological construct' on the other. However, most of those who use the test, or base their decisions on its outcomes, are unlikely to be fully aware of the remarkable implications of this distinction.' - from page 87 of The Technical Manual for the Hare Psychopathy Check List (Revised) (PCL-R): Second Edition. (July 2005, see www.mhs.com).

'Legal authorities and prison personnel, especially parole boards and other tribunals, understandably crave reliable indications that the person under their current scrutiny presents a low risk of re-offending. Indeed so great is the pressure for reassurance in this respect that corners are routinely cut, and expediencies deployed which, if given time for cool reflection, would be seen to be unacceptable, indeed to be quite illogical and entirely incompatible with any conceivable professional standard.'

'Risk assessment, as its name implies, sets out to be a measure of what that individual might do in the months and years to come. As such, it is an attempt to foretell the future — never an easy exercise in any context — though, given their statutory duty of protecting the public, society's many tribunals are regularly confronted with precisely this challenge. Not an easy burden. The reader has only to think about what he or she will be doing in say, a year's time, to gain some notion of the size of the problem. This is an important consideration — it will be obvious that all and every future decision will be based on two main factors — the circumstances you then find yourself in, and the plans, intentions or strategies you wished to implement. It takes no great scientific insight to see that all future human activities represent a blend between these two — circumstance and intention.

'Indeed such a supine approach to this ubiquitous test and its provenance appears entirely uncharacteristic of the legal profession. Expert witnesses can be subjected to harassment of a painfully detailed nature, as I can testify from my experience — yet here we have a test designed for one purpose — to establish the presence or absence of a 'construct' - namely 'psychopathy' — being used for entirely another, namely to assess the risk of future anti-social behaviour. Could it be, as one barrister assured me, that judges have already decided that 'once a psychopath always a psychopath'?'

Dr Johnson goes on to discuss the points that are relevant to clinical practice and the patient:

'Two points are relevant. The be-all and end-all of clinical practice is benefit to the patient — just as the fundamental objective of the criminal justice system is to protect the public safety and ensure fairness and justice for all. In clinical terms therefore, any concepts, constructs or nostrums you elect to deploy may be as eccentric, esoteric or eclectic as you wish — if they fulfil the essential criteria of benefiting the patient to whom they are applied, then however far they depart from the established orthodoxy, they should be given space to justify themselves.'

Johnson is well qualified to criticize the PCL-R. He is a practising psychiatrist and also Consultant Psychiatrist to the special Unit at Parkhurst Prison on the Isle of Wight, UK. His paper finishes with a case study of an individual and also mentions the Home office study mentioned in this chapter: 'Again, after the last 6 years, the Home Office denies the result of a PCL-R test is a diagnosis. That in identifying DSPD, which they now offer treatment for, DSPD is not a diagnosis gained from the use of PCL-R. (http://www.truthtrustconsent.com/public_html/law/pcl-r)

EARLY WARNING SIGNS OF FRAUD

When occupational fraud is detected in companies, it is usually by accident; someone notices something odd and investigates. The Association of Certified Fraud Examiners believes the main frauds are discovered by whistle-blowing. For more on whistle-blowing and the ACFE, see chapter 10. The author's contention, from his research, remains as stated above, that most frauds are discovered by accident. This accidental discovery of an oddity or anomaly does then translate into whistle-blowing. Sometimes fraud is detected by internal audit. Many cases go undetected for years before the perpetrator finally gets caught, usually because the fraudster makes a mistake or simply becomes complacent, thereby prompting an investigation. In most cases there are early warning signs that are not purposely ignored, but are seen for what they may mean. This is because business owners and company directors are not, per se, on the lookout for occupational fraud; they trust their employees. As an example, an employee who repeatedly comes in early, leaves late and works some weekends and holidays for no apparent reason may be seen by management as being keen to please, a good employee. In reality he is merely using the additional time to carry out his fraud and attempting to cover his tracks by falsifying company records.

EARLY WARNING SIGNS - ACCOUNTANTS

Accountants and audit companies will generally define several telltale signs that could indicate that an employee may be less than trustworthy. The commonly-accepted signs by accountants are as follows:

1) Arriving early, leaving late.
2) Working weekends and holidays for no apparent reason.
3) Not taking holidays.
4) Expensive cars for himself and family members.
5) Expensive holidays to exotic locations.
6) Moving into an expensive house or having a mini mansion built.

Typical company early warning signs:
1) Rising costs without explanation.
2) Unexplained margin erosion.
3) Unexplained or unexpected cash-flow problems.
4) Suppliers insisting on dealing with one employee.
5) No audit checks on new employees.
6) Employees with external business interests.
7) Customer complaints, missing statements.

EARLY WARNING SIGNS - PSYCHOLOGISTS

Psychologists who have experience of occupational fraudsters may well add to the early warning signs listed by the accounting profession. Consider the following: An angry employee who is a compulsive liar and a bully takes advantage of his/her position, is critical of other staff, bends the rules and does not conform. He or she would also be quick-tempered, exploitive and manipulative. Most employers would not suspect that an employee with the characteristics in the above sentences would pose a possible threat in terms of occupational fraud. Employers in general do not distrust their employees unless they have been given cause. Splitting out the characteristics and awarding marks in line with the key below could indicate a possible problem that would justify further investigation. These questions should be addressed to a close colleague and analysed by a professional with experience in the field of corporate criminality.

Is the person:

1)   Angry?

2)   A compulsive or pathological liar?

3)   The corporate bully?

4)   Critical of all other staff, regardless of position in the hierarchy?

5)   Quick tempered?

6)   Exploitative?

7)   Manipulative at all levels?

Does he/she:

8)   Take advantage of his/her position?

6)   Bend the company rules?

7)   Refuse to conform?

Score as follows: Characteristic never present, score 0. Present some of the time, score 1. Always present - score 2. A score of ten or more would indicate the need for a professional assessment of the employee in question.

The ten questions above are taken from the author's 76 questions used in his research. The questions which were not in sequence but randomised were later analysed with an appropriate analysis spread sheet.

Of all the accountants interviewed either formally or in informal conversations, only two, both Americans, were prepared to give credence to the above test. However, Clarke in *Working with Monsters* suggests a similar approach:

The following is an example of a questionnaire that can be given to as many people who know the job applicant as possible. The questionnaire is very similar to a traditional 360-degree review;

however the questions are designed to specifically assess workplace psychopath and antisocial type behaviours in the organisational setting. Scores are tallied at the end. If the applicant scores within a certain pattern or range, this suggests that additional investigation is necessary. Some sample questions from a total of ninety include:

1   Does ——— take responsibility for their behaviour?

2   Has ——— ever played one person against another in your office?

3   Has ——— ever had an affair to your knowledge with a person they work with?

4   Does ——— constantly look for new things to excite them?

5   Would you say that ——— has career aspirations that are realistic?

6   Has——— ever taken credit for work that you or someone else has done?

7   Has——— ever been on performance review or some other form of management plan?

8. Is ——— prepared to do whatever it takes to get what they want, regardless of the cost to

10. Does ——— ever act without thinking about the consequences of their behaviour?

12.   Does——— ever lose their temper for short periods of time to make people fraid of them?

13.   Who do you think is the most important person in ———'s life?

The rationale behind asking people other than the job applicant about previous performance is to get as balanced a view as possible. One drawback of using this questionnaire is that it is sometimes difficult to find previous colleagues who are willing to provide answers. This is not necessarily because the applicant is a workplace psychopath. It may be that the applicant has not informed their employer they are applying for a new job, colleagues may be difficult to find or approach discreetly, and many colleagues simply do not have the time to complete the questionnaire. A good consultant who is experienced in the area should have developed appropriate systems to circumvent these problems.

(*Working with Monsters*, P 239/240)

With the catalogue of early warning signs detailed above it is hard to believe that such people are not recognised for what they could be by managers. Are such fraudsters therefore extremely clever, or just lucky? Possibly neither applies. Management typically are not on the lookout for fraudsters in their organisations; they trust their employees. Why would a top manager not trust a plausible chartered accountant who is not only in a responsible position but is trusted?

When considering all the facts it is not surprising therefore that less than 10% of occupational frauds are reported to the authorities. To illustrate the apathy that exists when considering reporting occupational fraud, below is a quote from the 2004 Norwich Union Fraud Report:

'Most UK insurers (and many banks) no longer report the majority of frauds detected by them to the police, due to the very low historic take up rates. For example, in 2004 Norwich Union detected approximately 4,000 frauds with evidence levels that they believed to satisfy the test of 'beyond all reasonable doubt'. Of these, only 41 were considered likely to be accepted by the police on the basis of either significant public interest, involvement of organised crime or extraordinarily high levels of evidence. Of these 41 'super frauds' submitted, 27 were investigated, with 18 coming to Court. All 18 prosecutions subsequently resulted in convictions. However more than half resulted in a non-custodial sentence. (NU 2004)

DIFFICULTY IN DIAGNOSING PERSONALITY DISORDERS

The authors' research into occupational fraud looked into psychopathy associated with corporate criminality. Specifically the research was looking at traits and characteristics that would indicate personality disorders. During this research it became apparent that psychologists and psychiatrists might have difficulty diagnosing accurately the personality disorders of perpetrators of occupational fraud. In only four cases researched was it established that a diagnosis had been obtained. Of the four cases, a criminal psychologist had diagnosed one as suffering from Narcissistic Personality Disorder. Two had been diagnosed as sociopaths. With the fourth, management attested that their perpetrator had been described as 'a possible psychopath but maybe a narcissistic psychopath'. Management appeared to be somewhat vague as to the qualifications and experience of their expert. He had apparently made his statement following discussions with members of senior staff who had related behavioural patterns.

A high percentage of perpetrators had been observed by management and staff interviewed to exhibit behavioural patterns and characteristics associated with personality disorders. Additionally, early warning signs were identified in one hundred percent of companies interviewed, while the vast majority of companies interviewed had instances of early warning signs typical of those listed by almost any accounting firm.

The research was more interested in early warning signs that would be identified by psychologists. Such signs would be irritable behaviour, secretive actions, manipulation of co-workers, the corporate bully, the angry employee with a short fuse, the compulsive or pathological liar and the Jekyll and Hyde character. Identification of these characteristic behaviours would add to the likely diagnosis of personality disorder.

There was no attempt to diagnose; a true diagnosis would require that as well as observed characteristic traits, the subject would need to be seen by a qualified psychologist. However, when many characteristics were reported and marked in the questionnaire, the possibility of a diagnosis would seem to be likely.

It became apparent that several of the perpetrators of occupational fraud exhibited characteristic traits that seemed to blur the possibility of a firm diagnosis. There were several instances where it appeared that the perpetrator exhibited all nine characteristics of an NPD and would also score high on the Hare PCL-R test. These perpetrators would also exhibit, almost by default, some of the characteristics of Anti-Social Personality Disorder (APD), blurring the image further. Further research into this apparent blurred line in diagnosis resulted in the discovery that with NPDs in particular there is rarely a clear diagnosis.

The personality defects referred to in DSM-1V share some common traits, and indeed the term narcissistic psychopath is used in some papers on the subject. Some psychologists refer to such white-collar criminals as sociopaths, a term which does not have the same stigma as psychopath. This description is really defining a psychopath, but courts in particular shy away from using the term as it is generally associated with serial killers and serial rapists. One description of white-collar criminals describes a sociopath as a socialised psychopath. This in itself would seem extremely unlikely as how, if the personality traits as described in DSM-1V are considered, can a person with such characteristics become socialised?

One of the best descriptions, which addresses the confusion and sometimes incorrect use of terminology, is in John Clarke's book *Working with Monsters*:

> The terms psychopath, sociopath and anti-social personality disorder are often used incorrectly. Each of these terms describes the same general pattern of behaviour, but each label has subtle and important differences concerning cause and diagnosis. Clinicians and researchers who believe that social factors are exclusively responsible for the pattern of behaviours demonstrated by the individual use the term sociopath. Anti-Social Personality Disorder is a term used in DSM-1V, used by mental health professionals to describe a persistent, maladaptive behavioural pattern that occurs across the lifespan. Psychopath, on the other hand, refers to a syndrome of personality and behavioural characteristics. The term psychopath also suggests that the syndrome is caused by psychological, biological, generic and social factors rather that the social factor alone.

Whilst recognizing this description by Clarke, it does not help when many dictionaries define a sociopath as 'the same as psychopath' but without the stigma.

It is not surprising therefore with confusion of terminology, when trying to accurately describe a perpetrator of occupational fraud that the characteristic traits seem blurred at best. The issue becomes even more complicated when considering the four subdivisions of psychopaths often found in the corporate environment (Clarke 2005):

1) The organizational psychopath.
2) The corporate criminal psychopath.
3) The violent criminal psychopath.
4) The occupational psychopath.

Each of the subtypes is defined as having clusters of characteristic traits but all within the Hare PCL-R, so it is clear that overlaps will occur. Profession and lifestyle also figure in categorising. Certain individuals may migrate from one subset to another, thereby blurring diagnosis even further.

The author's research into occupational fraud found several examples of industrial psychopaths with a narcissistic style and also clear cases of NPDs who exhibited all nine characteristics but equally scored high in PCL-R. Findings seen in this research into occupational fraudsters clearly show that in many cases the diagnosis would be definitely blurred and in a few cases the possibility of multiple personality looked likely. Such criminals, by the very nature of their characteristic traits, could and have, in certain cases researched, become violent psychopaths and distinctly anti-social in their behaviour following detection. Regardless of accurate diagnosis of employee fraudsters and indeed their motivations, both industrial psychopaths and narcissists can, and often do, cause significant psychological and emotional damage to co-workers.

If diagnosis of these personality disorders is at best blurred, then how can psychologists be sure when diagnosing an occupational fraudster? One possibility when trying to define the difference between an industrial psychopath and a narcissist would be to try to establish if the perpetrator was naturally a person with no or low self-esteem. This is difficult to establish, as NPDs rarely let other people see their true self. Nevertheless low personal esteem in reality would more than likely establish the perpetrator as NPD as opposed to being a psychopath.

One UK company researched stated that a criminal psychologist diagnosed their perpetrator as an NPD. Six months after his dismissal he joined another company. Within a year he had his fingers in the till again and was summarily dismissed, but once more the authorities were not informed. The reasons given were that both companies did not wish to endure the bad publicity associated with court cases. In both these companies the perpetrator had exhibited many of the early warning signs identified by industrial psychologists.

When interviewing victim companies of occupational fraud the researcher was told of many incidents which could lightly be described as bullying. In some cases the employee was clearly exhibiting narcissistic rage and becoming aggressive and violent. In these cases there were also strong indications of blurred definition of a diagnosis or multiple personality disorders. Martha Stout, in her book: The Sociopath next door, states: 'I have learned that the damage caused by the sociopath among us is deep and lasting, often tragically lethal and startlingly common' (Stout 2005).

When considering the characteristic traits of NPDs, psychopaths and of anti-social personality disorder (appended), it becomes easier to understand not only the blurring of diagnosis but the possibility of multiple personality disorders. The definitions given in DSM-1V of anti-social personality disorder have themselves come under criticism. Robert Hare and some other renowned psychologists are critical of the DSM-1V definition of APD.

In 1999 the British Government released a consultation document that had many psychiatrists and indeed civil rights campaigners protesting. The document title was 'Managing Dangerous People with Severe Personality Disorders'. This document proposed that such people could be detained using mental health law on the grounds of public protection, whether or not they had committed a crime (HMSO 1999). After years of debate the mental health bill now before Parliament has changed some of the proposed wording. It removes the 'treatability' test and in its place has used the term that 'appropriate treatment should be available'. The House of Lords amended the bill in response to complaints, but the government intends to push the original version through the House of Commons.

In deciding which violent offenders to treat, UK officials devised a complex set of criteria to define exactly what DSPD actually is. Offenders eligible for this new controversial treatment must be deemed more than likely to commit future offences that could cause serious harm from which victims would find it difficult or impossible to recover. They must have a severe personality disorder and a link between that disorder and the risk of violent offending (HMSO 1999).

DSPD for this experimental treatment is defined in the white paper as:

- A score of 30 or above on the Hare PCL-R.
- A PCL-R score of 25 to 29 plus diagnosis of at least one personality disorder other than anti-social personality disorder.
- Two or more diagnosed personality disorders.

About 130 offenders have been enrolled in this DSPD programme, based in specialised units in two prisons and two secure hospitals. The programme is intended to eventually include 300 subjects. A team headed by Tom Burns and Jenny Yiend of the University of Oxford will evaluate its success. Initial results are expected by 2009.

There is also controversial treatment taking place at a specialised unit within Franklin prison in Durham UK. This treatment is looking at treating so called DSPDs (Dangerous Severe Personality Disorder) but specialises in psychopaths, and it is attracting much interest from forensic psychiatrists. The subjects are being subjected to a most intensive treatment plan. This newly devised plan is known as 'Chromis' and employs both individual and group therapy. Its purpose is to shift ingrained patterns of thought and behaviour. All staff members in the unit are used to ensure that the subjects are subjected to a continuous exercise in cognitive-behavioural therapy as opposed to simply relying on short sessions. Psychopaths usually refuse treatment as they do not acknowledge that they have a behavioural problem - how can they, as they have no 'conscience'? (Hare 1993)

Perpetrators of occupational fraud are not usually violent, but they do frequently reoffend. Research into this subject has seen many cases of perpetrators reoffending. Where the victim company goes to the authorities they are then found to have served time for similar offences. Such men and women will not accept that they have any personality disorders or indeed have done anything wrong. They have an overwhelming sense of entitlement and rarely admit to any of their indiscretions. Are such individuals therefore exhibiting characteristic behaviour indicating personality disorder, or could they be described as suffering from a personality disorder?. Does a diagnosis by a psychologist or a psychiatrist indicate that the person is suffering from the condition? If they are sufferers, can they be treated or cured? Is the syndrome a mental illness, as in a psychopathic disorder? In the UK Mental Health Act amended in 1982, a psychopathic disorder is defined as: 'a persistent disorder or disability of mind (whether or not including significant impairment of intelligence) which results in abnormally aggressive or seriously irresponsible conduct'.

There is no doubt that psychopaths and narcissistic personality disordered individuals carrying out occupational fraud fit the qualification cited above. They can therefore be defined as exhibiting signs of a psychiatric disorder, or indeed be diagnosed. It is beyond the scope of this research to delve into the above questions, as the subjects are complex and interdependent. The researcher however looked into the possibility of treatment of such disorders. In none of the cases investigated, where the perpetrators had been professionally diagnosed, had there been any discussion about treatment.

Jessica Lee in *The Treatment of Psychopathic and Anti-Social Personality Disorders* states: 'Personality disorders are defined as deeply ingrained and enduring attitude and behaviour patterns that deviate markedly from the culturally expected range. They are not secondary to other mental illnesses, or attributable to gross brain damage or disease, although they may precede and coexist with other disorders. Disorders of personality are regarded as developmental conditions which tend to appear in late childhood or adolescence and continue to manifest into adulthood. Diagnosis of a personality disorder, therefore, would not usually be appropriate before the age of sixteen years, although the presence of conduct disorder during childhood or adolescence can indicate a predisposition towards the syndrome'.

Lee discusses all the personality disorders looked into in this research and describes various treatments, along with many quotations from eminent experts in the field. It is however her conclusions on her research into treating psychopathic disorders that are worthy of note in this research, as they help to put into perspective the difficulties in dealing with personality disorders. She writes:

> The general criteria for recommending the transfer or discharge of a mentally disordered patient who is serving a hospital order is that there should be sufficient psychological change (either an amelioration of psychiatric symptoms, or personality difficulties), so that the patient no longer requires protection from the public (Grounds, 1987). The research on the treatment of psychopathic patients, however, suggests that those working with this group have experienced considerable

difficulty in reducing the complex spread of psychiatric symptoms and core personality deficiencies associated with this disorder. Arguably, the research material in this area is scarce and of poor methodological quality, with few experiments using controls and adequate follow-up periods and too many relying upon recidivism statistics as a measure of success, when these are notoriously inaccurate. It has also been difficult to make comparisons between the different studies carried out in this field, because so many of them use different diagnostic criteria for their subjects and monitor their progress with incompatible assessment devices.

Lee in her conclusion also points out the difficulty in treatment and the reluctance of many institutions to take on treatment on the grounds that such individuals are 'untreatable'. The Government is however following the experiments detailed in this chapter in more controlled environments with multi treatment procedures.

Lee also states: 'Some believe that the nature of the psychopathic condition is such that clinicians cannot be expected to change the behaviour of those suffering with the syndrome. Arguably, psychopathy is characterised by behavioural features which, in themselves, imply the failure of the individual to respond to normal sanctions on his or her behaviour. If others have failed to effect change in the individual, perhaps then it is unreasonable to expect psychiatrists or psychologists to be able to do so'.

Not only is there difficulty in a pure diagnosis of personality disorders; there is seemingly equal difficulty in treating the syndrome. Whilst there may not be any physical violence in occupational fraud, there is no doubt that victim managers suffer emotionally and psychologically as a result of having trusted perpetrators. Victim managers often state 'It's not only the money it is the betrayal of trust'. Although it is unlikely to be proven, there are many victims who blame the stress caused by such criminals for triggering latent medical conditions (Warrington 2007).

There is no doubt that employee fraud causes grief and sometimes lasting emotional and psychological damage to victim managers. To add to this grief, invariably there is no diagnosis of perpetrators, merely suggestions. There is however the lingering question: What kind of person sinks to these levels? Answer, probably an industrial psychopath.

DISCOVERY OF FRAUD

How are occupational fraudsters discovered? Usually by accident, that is to say someone notices an oddity or simply has a gut feeling that something, usually with the numbers, is not as it should be. Current research suggests that most occupational frauds are discovered by accident. Sometimes the perpetrators are found out by internal audit, but this is almost as rare as whistle-blowing. Either a whistle-blower or a staff member who has noticed an oddity and become suspicious sparks the need for an internal audit. One company investigated originally suggested that the fraudster had been found out by an internal audit exercise. During the interview with the manager it became apparent that he had indeed called in the internal audit team after an employee had noticed that there was an anomaly in some paperwork that he had been asked to review. The internal audit team discovered the detail and the perpetrator was fired, but the original suspicion was from the employee. This could be called whistle-blowing, but this company and others interviewed do not like the expression.

Some large companies try to implement not only sophisticated anti-fraud measures and policies but other tools designed to encourage detection and in particular whistle-blowing. Such measures would include 360-degree evaluation, anonymous reporting of colleagues and managers and matrix management.

360-degree evaluation is simply where employees are encouraged on a regular basis, say annually, to evaluate their co-workers and managers.

Anonymous reporting is used extensively in some organisations as the main weapon against employee fraud. This method is in fact encouraged whistle-blowing. The researcher has been privileged to read documents used in one organisation where rules for this type of activity are laid down in great detail. These documents were shown on the understanding that none of the content or the organisations name would be used in this book.

Matrix management is used in many multinational organisations almost as a necessity. Put simply, matrix management is where employees have to report to more than one boss but in different areas of expertise. This is usually where large projects are undertaken on a global basis. These projects are typically managed by a person with the required qualifications and expertise. He will naturally have a line manager in headquarters. He will also have to report to the manager in the country where he is managing the project. Because of the nature of what he is managing, he will also probably have to report to a finance manager. If he is working on a technical project, then his personal expertise will not include finance. He may also have a divisional manager. The difference between matrix management and conventional functional management is in the number of bosses. In the normal hierarchy of business, functional management is where each employee reports to only one supervisor or manager. The divisions in companies would typically be; sales, marketing, engineering, finance, product development etc.

Project organisation is where the team has many levels of expertise and therefore has cross-functional expertise. Matrix management therefore combines both conventional functional management and project orientated management. One company that used all of the above methods was Enron (McLean and Elkind 2004).

Betrayal of trust

During the author's research into company and employee victims of occupational fraud, it became apparent that more investigation was required into trust and the betrayal of trust. From interviews with victims, it became clear that all perpetrators had been trusted - not only with company money and finances, but as co-workers and in many cases as friends.

Other emotions described by victims contribute to the overwhelming feelings of betrayal. The denial felt by most victims, with total disbelief that such a trusted employee could behave in this way, came through very strongly in the interviews. These feelings seem to be accompanied by a sense of stupidity for having bestowed trust on employees who in most cases had become friends over the years. The initial feelings of anger and the need for revenge are also mixed up in the victim's emotions. Some victims lost their confidence and some blamed themselves for allowing events to happen. These feelings in some directors made them feel that they had failed as businessmen.

All interviewees reported the devastating effect when they finally realised that they had been betrayed by highly-trusted employees. In many cases they first had to accept the truth of what had been discovered, sometimes after several months of being in denial. Many company owners and managers, whether at director level or not, could not come to terms with the basic facts; they had been taken in by employees who had been trusted with company money. This denial manifested itself in the firm belief that it was all a big mistake, and it was really incompetence that they were seeing in the figures in the management accounts.

It was clear that because of the psychological damage caused to victims' managers and colleagues, further investigation into trust was required.

What does trust really mean? The Oxford Dictionary on line defines trust as follows: 'Firm belief in the reliability, truth, ability or strength of someone, the acceptance of truth of a statement without evidence or investigation, and the state of being responsible'. Similarly, the verb 'trust' is defined as 'having the confidence to allow someone to have, use or look after'. (www.oxforddictionaries.com 2007)

This definition serves to explain why so many victims feel that they have been betrayed. *Trust in Society*, published by the Russell Sage foundation in New York, has much more to say about trust. This extract is from 'Conceptions of Trust', a review of the book by Karen Cook:

In the first chapter Hardin lays out a framework for analyzing current conceptions of trust. A major contribution of this chapter is that it also makes clear the distinction between trust and related concepts of trustworthiness, confidence, and the act of entrusting something to someone. In clarifying the conceptual ground he identifies several major confusions in the work on trust. Perhaps the most common flaw in much of the literature on trust is the failure to distinguish discussions of trust from discussions of trustworthiness. If everyone we interact with were trustworthy, there would be no problem of trust. Much of the concern with trust in the popular literature can best be understood as concern over the lack of trustworthiness in society. When we attempt to produce mechanisms for making people more trustworthy, we are trying to solve the problem of trust by creating conditions under which it is much less risky to trust. At the extremes, if you are 100 percent trustworthy, I would be taking no risk in leaving my valuables in your possession; the act of 'trusting' in this context is thus not at all problematic. (Cook 2003: xiv)

Trust is fundamental to society; without it, we could not function. In companies there has to be trust all round; employees trust their bosses and management trust their employees. This is a given fact and the process in business of promoting staff to take on more responsibilities is in fact an expression of trust. Where fraud occurs in a company there is always a betrayal of this trust.

How do organisations avoid the problem? In short, they do not. They never really expect to become victims, especially of trusted employees. In all the companies investigated, there was trust in the perpetrator before discovery. Four of the investigated companies were family owned and/or controlled. *Trust in Society* suggests how some family-owned businesses deal with this potential problem area:

'When the costs of misplaced trust are high, individuals often try to solve the problem of trust by relying on family members or other kin, assuming them to be more trustworthy than strangers. Embedding the act of trust in a network of social relations is a move that often reduces both uncertainty and vulnerability. It also increases the extent to which the trusted has an incentive to fulfil the trust. The use of family relations to 'solve' the problem of trust is so common that in some cultures it has been extended by creating kin like relations as the basis for trust in significant economic endeavours'. (Cook 2003: xix)

In all the family companies investigated there was total trust in family members. It has to be said however that none of the cases indicated that they had hired relatives to reduce the risk of fraud. In all cases they never envisaged fraud in their businesses. The subject had never been highlighted and therefore was not seen as a potential threat.

The feeling that trust has been betrayed is in fact a natural reaction to the exposure of a fraudster, especially one who had been a colleague and also a friend. On the website whitecollarfraud.com, Sam Antar, a convicted fraudster, had this to say with respect to trust in the way of advice to the accounting profession, anti-fraud professionals and Wall Street. This statement was apparently given in front of District Judge Nicholas H Politan by Sam Antar immediately prior to sentencing on May 27 1994.

1) Do not trust, just verify, verify and verify.

2) White-collar criminals build a wall of false integrity around them to gain the trust of their victims.

3) White-collar criminals measure their effectiveness by the comfort level of their victims.

4) White-collar criminals consider your humanity, ethics, and good intentions as a weakness to be exploited in the execution of their crimes.

5) White-collar crime can be more brutal than violent crime, since white-collar crime imposes a collective harm on society.

6) No criminal finds morality and stops committing crime simply because another criminal went to jail.

Sam Antar, a convicted felon, is now a lecturer on white-collar fraud and owner of the web site www.whitecollarfraud.com.

Research indicated that in many small to medium sectors of UK companies, significant anti-fraud policies are not in place. Most companies interviewed had simple policies. Even where policies and basic procedures are in place, they are not regularly monitored. Many small companies (less than £5,000,000 turnover) argue, quite rightly, that instituting such policies is by default, saying to their employees that they are not trusted. This is seen as counterproductive, particularly in small and family-controlled companies employing fewer than 100 staff. Yet some companies go out of business because of the resultant cash flow problems. These companies typify the ones that do not get reported. In many cases the events of discovery and the subsequent investigation by forensic auditors adds to the insult. Betrayal of trust and the subsequent feelings of failure on the part of owners and management would appear to add to the emotional and psychological damage caused by occupational fraud.

The research showed that in all companies researched, there had been many and varied early warning signs. This opinion is endorsed by conversations with several accountants who had experienced occupational fraud with some of their clients. Signs have not been purposely ignored; they have not been recognised for what they are. Examples include arriving early and leaving late, working weekends when there is no apparent need and not taking holidays other than the odd days, all typically seen as traits of a keen employee. They are also the signs that audit companies always describe as telltale signs of possible operational fraudsters. Other signs identified by accounting firms would include a lavish lifestyle and owning expensive motor-cars. Corporate signs identified by interviewing victim companies indicate the two most obvious company signs, but not always recognised by management as early warning signs; these are unexplained margin erosion and unexplained and unexpected cash flow problems.

PSYCHOLOGISTS' WARNING SIGNS

Examination of some of the more obscure early warning signs could facilitate a better understanding of the personalities that might typify perpetrators of occupational fraud. Signs identified by industrial psychologists such as Dr Paul Babiak, an industrial psychologist working in New York, include the corporate bully, the employee who is a pathological or compulsive liar, the angry employee (short fuse), and the employee who is manipulative and is always sucking up to directors and management in a smooth talking but convincing manner. (Babiak and Hare 2006). Abrupt changes in character are another warning sign; companies interviewed by the author often describe the perpetrator as being a Jekyll and Hyde person. Comments are made to the effect that it is as if someone has turned a switch - one minute the person was normal, the next a bad-tempered, obnoxious foul-mouthed bully.

Such perpetrators are often suffering from severe

personality disorders. Disorders include the psychopath (sociopath) referred to as industrial psychopaths by Babiak, co-author of *Snakes in Suits*. Hare, Babiak's co-author, is recognised as a leading authority on psychopaths and his PCL-R method of testing for them is used worldwide by psychologists to identify and diagnose such people. (Babiak and Hare 2006).

Narcissistic personality disorder (NPD) is another personality disorder often found in perpetrators of corporate fraud. The psychology student will learn that both these personality traits share many attributes in common, so the line of differentiation is blurred. The term 'narcissistic psychopath' is used in some papers on the subject. Sam Vaknin, himself an NPD, is the author of *Malignant Self Love-Narcissism Revisited* and uses this term. Sam was diagnosed as an NPD whilst serving time in an Israeli jail after being convicted on fraud-related charges. Sam, in an interview for Radio National Australia on the subject of 'psychopaths in suits', states:

'Many narcissists are also psychopaths and most psychopaths also have narcissistic traits, or a narcissistic style, or even a narcissistic personality, so the distinctions are blurred, and many people think they are artificial. There's very rarely a pure diagnosis of narcissism'. (Vaknin 2009)

Personality refers to patterns of feelings and thoughts as well as behavioural traits. These factors shape the personalities of all of us. We are all different and display various characteristics depending on the circumstances and the company of people with whom we find ourselves. People don't always feel, think and behave in exactly the same way, even in the same situations. In general people tend to behave reasonably and in predictable ways. They can therefore be described in general terms, for example arrogant, shy, reserved, funny, boring, friendly etc. Each person exhibits the characteristic traits which shape their personality.

Personality disorders can therefore be described as variations or exaggerations of normal personality traits and behaviour. Personality disorders are often associated with antisocial behaviour, but most people with diagnosable personality disorders do not act or display anti-social behaviour. On the other hand some people with diagnosed personality disorders such as narcissistic personality disorder and the psychopath or sociopath can exhibit some signs of anti-social behaviour. One of the personality disorders described in DSM-1V is Anti-Social Personality Disorder. ASPD can be and often is linked to adult criminal behaviour.

If we accept that many people with these disorders are highly intelligent, well-qualified individuals, it may surprise many to learn that such people are manipulative and lack empathy for other human beings, and also 'have no conscience'. In *Without Conscience* Hare has this to say about trust when referring to a specific white-collar psychopath: 'Mr ——— was able to use his charm, social skills and family connections, to gain the trust of others. He was aided by the common expectation that certain classes of people presumably are trustworthy because of their credentials.'

Hare goes on to say: 'In most cases trust is not misplaced, but the very fact that we are so willing to give it makes us easy prey for every opportunist shark that we encounter. Most dangerous of all, the Jaws of the trust mongers are psychopaths. Having obtained our trust, they betray our trust; they betray it with stunning callousness.' (Hare 1993)

TRUST IN SOCIETY

If we consider what Hare and other eminent psychologists have to say about white-collar criminals, it becomes easier to understand the damage caused to the owners and managers of victim companies. Betrayal of trust in society is a fundamental betrayal. Complex societies need trust in order to function. Trust is naturally taken for granted; most companies, institutions and fundamental relationships in our society rely on it. What would our society be without trust? We all trust others naturally, and cannot function effectively without trusting people and institutions. We all trust our doctors, surgeons and anaesthetists when we undergo surgery. We trust our banks to take care of our money. We all trust each other.. The betrayal of this trust by perpetrators of occupational fraud is therefore a severe blow to our naturally trusting nature.

We cannot go through our lives distrusting everyone;

we could not function in society in this mode, and nothing would get done. The trusting manager, business owner or company director therefore suffers when this fundamental trust is betrayed.

This research in the UK and the USA has concluded that in many cases there has been significant damage to the victim manager. Other than extreme emotional and psychological damage, some cases are believed to have triggered severe illness in victims. Examples discussed at interviews include depression, nervous breakdowns and stress-related medical conditions. There were several interviewees who were convinced that the stress caused by occupational fraudsters had caused medical conditions such as stress-induced diabetes, cancer and stress-related heart conditions. Also with some women interviewed, miscarriages were blamed on the stress caused by fraudsters.

The feeling of failure for not having seen what was happening is a common comment made by victim managers interviewed. 'How could he/she do this to me?', 'I trusted him/her' are typical of statements made during interviews. Many interviewees state: 'It's not the money, I feel let down, I really trusted him.' Others have commented, 'Why would I not trust a chartered accountant?' For many and varied reasons victim managers find justification for not bringing in the authorities. Typical reasons are the bad publicity that will follow – 'He only got away with £X,000, the company will survive.' In cases where the resultant cash flow causes the company to fail, interviewees initially want revenge and then they become depressed or worse, particularly in the company where the director concerned is the owner/founder or indeed a significant shareholder. The thought of adding to the hurt by going through a trial and months of meetings of preparation is also a strong deterrent. One victim interviewed indicated that his lawyer had advised against legal action on the grounds that he had suffered enough and 'did he really want up to two years of added grief with no guarantee of a conviction or a return of the money?'

If we accept that the damage is more than just the money, then what does the law have to say about, not the theft, but the betrayal of trust and larceny itself?

In medieval times larceny was a capital offence. The well-known piece of medieval literature Dante's *Inferno* discusses betrayal:

'In the Inferno, those who suffer in the ninth circle are all guilty of betrayal. Their common sin described as the intentional betrayal or deception of friends, family and/or country. In Dante's afterlife such betrayals of trust are seen as the most serious of crimes, worse than sins of passion and even acts of violence. The Inferno argues that acts of deliberate betrayal of duty to others tears at the social fabric and therefore damages society more significantly than other so called violent crimes.' (Kobrin 2006:8)

This research investigated only four family-owned companies of the many identified, many refusing to be interviewed.

Modern law sees the betrayal of trust somewhat differently from in medieval times; violent crimes, rape and murder are seen as justifying long prison sentences. There is no appropriate legal charge for betrayal of trust as such, but dereliction of fiduciary duty by a director or manager may result in a charge being brought. The law appears to sentence fraud-related crime to a large extent on a scale that would seem to be related to the amount of money stolen, in other words the higher the sum the longer the sentence.

EXAMPLES OF CORPORATE FRAUD

ENRON

As an example of a long sentence, Andy Fastow, the creative accountant working for Enron, was facing a minimum of thirty years for his part in the Enron affair. Initially he was going to fight all 98 counts of his indictment. Later he agreed or was persuaded by his council to admit to two counts in exchange for a reduced sentence of ten years without parole. This reduced sentence, the result of a plea bargain, was after Fastow agreed to help the authorities and testify against other Enron executives. Part of the deal was his agreement to pay back almost 24m dollars, most of which was already frozen in various accounts. Even though this reduced sentence was a federal agreement, meant to be non-contestable on an appeal, Fastow's lawyers managed to create sympathy with an appeal court judge and his sentence was reduced to six years. The judge, Kenneth Hoyt, remarked that Fastow had already paid a heavy price for his actions: 'Prosecution is necessary not persecution' (Enron Trials 2002-2006). Fastow's wife went to jail for a year, again following a plea bargain, for her part in helping Fastow hide his ill-gotten gains.

The Enron case is a good example of judges not accepting the hurt done to others by occupational fraudsters. No consideration is given to the suffering of thousands of Enron employees, who not only lost their jobs but their pensions.

A good example of pension fund victims in the UK is of course the Robert Maxwell Mirror Group scandal. Maxwell's betrayal of the trust vouchsafed to him by his company and workforce is a classic example of such a case. It is worth a more detailed explanation than Enron, as it was a UK company.

The Mirror Group and the Robert Maxwell Scandal - the 1971 DTI Report

In 1971 inspectors appointed by the DTI produced a report on Pergamon Press Ltd, which was severely critical of Mr Robert Maxwell. They concluded: 'We regret having to conclude that, notwithstanding Mr Maxwell's acknowledged abilities and energy, he is not in our opinion a person who can be relied on to exercise

proper stewardship of a publicly quoted company.'
(DTI 1971)

In two subsequent reports on Pergamon Press Ltd
and related companies in 1972/73 the same inspectors
detailed and criticised Mr Robert Maxwell's business
methods. Notwithstanding these reports by the DTI,
Maxwell was allowed to go on and build an empire that
finally collapsed in 1991. This collapse of a significant
UK listed group caused the loss of many jobs and also
cost thousands of Mirror Group employees their
pensions. All these employees and their families were in
effect white-collar victims.

The following summary of events leading to the
collapse of the Maxwell Empire is taken from the 2001
DTI report on the Mirror Group.

Cash was borrowed by the private side of Maxwell
companies on a regular and unsecured basis from the
pension funds beginning in 1985. This did not become
known to the trustees of the funds. The accounts were
'window dressed' with balances brought to nil at the
financial year end to avoid disclosure. The pension funds
were used on a regular basis to assist in the corporate
strategy of the empire and to provide cash in exchange
for investments which Maxwell Communication
Corporation or other businesses needed to sell. The
pension funds made substantial investments in Maxwell
Communication Corporation shares. The presentation of
the financial position of Mr Robert Maxwell's companies

and the pension funds in the annual accounts was carefully managed and the minimum disclosure made.

The DTI report itemises the events leading up to the collapse of the group. This report starts in 1986 when pension funds were first used by Maxwell.

When Mirror Group Newspapers needed £34m cash in 1986, this was provided by the pension funds in return for shares held by Mirror Group Newspapers in Reuters. When these shares were transferred back in 1989, the pension funds not only made a loss on the transaction, but never obtained any part of the significant profits which the private side earned when the Reuters share price increased very shortly thereafter. The pension funds were used to purchase Maxwell House in Holborn, London in 1986, but it was the private side that obtained the real benefits on the transaction.

As Robert Maxwell had always regarded the pension funds as his, when financial pressures on his companies became greater in 1988, he made greater use of the pension funds through the practices identified in paragraph 6. Some banks became reluctant to accept Maxwell Communication Corporation shares as collateral for loans to the private side, because they would in effect be taking, for a loan to one group of companies controlled by Maxwell, collateral from another company controlled by him.

From November 1988, Maxwell therefore began to

make use of the more marketable blue chip shares held by the pension funds and First Tokyo Index Trust as collateral for bank borrowings to the private side; this was described as 'stock lending' to make it appear to be the legitimate practice of lending securities to market makers as part of ordinary share dealing activities. Cash continued to be borrowed from the pension funds by the private side without providing any collateral to the pension funds for these loans. A significant part of the shares of the pension funds and First Tokyo Index Trust which were used as collateral were held by an independent custodian. Maxwell ran his companies and the pension funds as if they were one. He moved assets between them as best suited his overall interests. However, the complex ownership and financial structure of his empire and the concealment of the use of the pension funds made it difficult for banks to gain a clear picture of the financial strength of his empire. The practice was to be 'economic with the information' supplied to them. Although all the groups of companies and pension funds within Maxwell's empire were audited, they were not audited at a common date. Nor was there any overview of the empire as a whole. By the end of October 1991, the private side, having made significant disposals, had no substantial assets other than shares in Mirror Group Newspapers and Maxwell Communication Corporation and property. At that time the pressures became severe. For example, Goldman Sachs required repayment of two loans. When repayment was not made, they began selling Maxwell Communication Corporation shares provided as collateral; the share price fell substantially. The directors of Mirror Group Newspapers were examining the use being made of about £40m of Mirror Group Newspapers' assets. Lehmans demanded repayment of their financing. It is apparent that Maxwell could not seek the support of his bankers to save his empire without disclosing the true state of affairs and the use he had made of the pension funds. The imminent collapse of the empire was inevitable. As a result of the collapse, many pensioners suffered anxiety and loss and the employees of Maxwell's companies suffered uncertainty and redundancy. Maxwell's son Kevin and others associated with Maxwell faced a long criminal trial in which they were acquitted. Disciplinary proceedings were brought by self-regulatory organisations.

Maxwell's total disregard for company rules, not to mention ethical considerations, was symptomatic of the man. He manipulated not only company accounts but, to a degree, his auditors. His sense of entitlement and total lack of empathy for others, coupled with his manipulative skills, indicate a psychopathic personality. Indeed in the documentary film *Psychopath* Maxwell is cited as an example of an industrial psychopath (CH 4 TV 2007). Maxwell's total disregard for company rules, not to mention ethical considerations, was symptomatic of the man. He manipulated not only company accounts, but also to a degree his auditors. His sense of entitlement and total lack of empathy for others, coupled with his manipulative skills, indicate a calculating and strong personality.

The author believes that the whole subject of occupational fraud and its victims is a neglected subject from an empirical research point of view. There is undoubtedly much room for additional research to be carried out on victims of white-collar crime and occupational fraud. The topic seems to have been somewhat neglected by academics/researchers, largely because so few cases are brought to the attention of the authorities, and of those that are reported only a small percentage result in custodial sentences.

CASE STUDY USA

The following simple yet tragic case illustrates the damage that can be caused by unscrupulous perpetrators of occupational fraud. The company in the United States was the so-called 'Ma and Pa Shop'. The couple had been in the same business for over forty years and had had a good but not excessive lifestyle when, in their early seventies, they hired a much younger man and gave him some shares in the business. They had picked him because they believed him to be talented. He told them what they wanted to hear and was extremely hard working. He never took any holidays and was always in work early.

There is a strong suspicion that this perpetrator picked

the elderly couple as he saw an opportunity - in a word, he conned them. They wanted him to run the business in order that eventually they could retire; his job was to build the company with a view to an eventual sale of the business. The shares in the company given to him would ensure that he was rewarded for his work following the sale. But over a period of several years he bled the company dry, and the company failed. The resultant investigation showed the owners that it was not the business that had gone down but the fraud carried out by the trusted employee that caused the cash-flow problem. The old couple blamed themselves and today are in their early eighties and both out at work in order to live.

In this case the perpetrator did go to jail, but no money was recovered. The couple gained no satisfaction from their perpetrator's jail sentence. They still cannot understand how he could do it to them; they were good to him and trusted him with their retirement plans and the business.

The couple paid the ultimate price of trust. The betrayal and the loss of their comfortable retirement took away their self-esteem. They both ended up doing menial tasks in Wal-Mart to earn enough money to live. (Brock 2007)

Victims of occupational fraud

In order to investigate the feelings and welfare of victims of occupational fraud there is a need to understand why the victims suffered. In many cases owners, directors, managers, employees, shareholders and families of these groups as well as families of perpetrators continue to suffer years after the trauma of discovering fraud. The discovery that the person they knew is not the person they thought he/she was but someone who was capable of stealing in many cases large sums of money is hard to understand and come to terms with. The betrayal of trust and all that it signifies is a fundamental betrayal (see Chapter 5). Coming to terms with the discovery that their colleague, employee, husband, wife or family member is not what they appeared to be, can and does cause in many victims, a deep psychological hurt or damage.

PYSCHOPATHY

Several well-known and respected academic psychologists have written books on the subject of psychopaths and people suffering from personality disorders. There have also been TV documentary programmes on industrial psychopaths. These books in the main look at industrial psychopaths and the havoc they can cause when they turn to monetary crime in business. They also try to make sense of the nature and causes of fraudulent behaviour.

Many of the victims interviewed in the author's research had been made aware for the first time of serious personality defects in their perpetrators. This was where perpetrators were reported to the authorities and subsequently jailed for their offences. This usually comes about as the defence lawyers request a psychiatric analysis in order to put up a defence on grounds of diminished responsibility. We should therefore consider the character of the perpetrator and where possible any personality traits that may be indicated by their behavioural characteristics, personality flaws or disorders.

Many of the victim managers interviewed were very concerned that in the company's investigations into the fraud the subject of personality disorders was raised. In some companies where the perpetrators had been prosecuted, court-appointed psychologists had diagnosed the perpetrators as suffering from personality disorders.

Two defined personality disorders, the NPD, (Narcissistic personality disorder) and the Psychopath or Sociopath were diagnosed by court appointed professionals in many of the cases studied.

Other groups where personality disorders have been noted is where there has been a divorce, following the discovery of fraud. In these cases, where court appointed psychologists or psychiatrists had diagnosed personality flaws, the husband or wife fraudster became extremely aggressive and threatening to his/her spouse. Restraining court orders had to be sought in order to safeguard the victims and their children. In all these cases there had been a diagnosis of personality defaults. These revelations do nothing to modify the feelings of disgust and betrayal in the victim's eyes, quite the reverse in many cases. The discovery that they had been working with or married to, for example, a person suffering from a psychopathic personality disorder adds further injury and hurt to the victims. The instances mentioned are factual, but looking further into the personalities of perpetrators is beyond the scope of this investigation. It could however be an additional topic that may be covered in future research. The author believes that this topic along with victims of white-collar crime is a somewhat neglected subject.

WHITE-COLLAR V. STREET CRIMINALS

The question remains as to the appropriateness of differentiating white-collar criminals and occupational fraudsters from other types of criminal. Is it too simplistic to argue that they are of a higher social status and educational level than, shall we say, street criminals? Many so-called 'street criminals' tend to be opportunistic and varied in their crimes, whereas occupational fraudsters undoubtedly plan not only their methods but also their way of disguising their actions by falsifying company accounts.

In Understanding Criminal Behaviour, Jones (2008) discusses in some detail differences between the professional white-collar criminal and street criminals. When discussing criminal careers, Jones quotes from Weisburd, Waring and Chayet 2001:

'They argue that the pattern of offending characteristic of white-collar crime is very different from those crimes more typically captured by the longitudinal studies (which might be referred to as street crime). White-collar crime tends to be committed by those who first offend well into adulthood and who are likely to be middle-class and relatively well educated, suggesting that this is a major problem for criminal career theorists. There are a couple of objectives to this analysis: first empirical evidence on the childhood and family backgrounds of white-collar criminals has not being gathered. It is possible that the lives of such offenders have been marked by antisocial behaviour and possibly family deprivation before adulthood; second, it may be that some similarity with patterns of street crime does emerge when the distinction is made between chronic and one off offender.

'However, Weisburd et al (2001) found that chronic white-collar offenders did not seem so different from more serious general offenders, deviance in the lives of those offenders is not restricted to criminality, but often appears to be the central part of their childhood development and adult histories such offenders are well described by common crime samples.' (Jones 2008:101)

The present research did not look into the backgrounds of occupational fraudsters, nor was it discussed with interviewees. It was apparent that the corporate fraudsters investigated had carried out their crimes on many occasions and used more than one fraudulent method over a period of years. The more devious ones were getting involved with many different devious practices and accounting system manipulation. In several of the cases researched there was evidence of having committed occupational fraud previously in other companies.

VICTIMS OF FRAUD AND OTHER FORMS OF CRIMINAL VIOLENCE

Victims of fraud, whether it is occupational fraud or any other form of fraud against a person, suffer both emotionally and psychologically following the discovery. These crimes have certain victim features in common with other victims of crime. Victims of rape, domestic violence and burglary all suffer with a number of common features, for example:

Personal fraud: The victims and the scams by Titus and Gover; 'the feelings of victims seem to equate well with victims of other crimes some of which are more violent. Public perceptions of crime as a social problem often depend, in part, on the specific type of crime being referred to. When thinking about or discussing crime, most people have images of violent street crime, such as robbery, assault, rape, etc. As a result, a large amount of research in criminology and criminal justice has focused on the financial and physical consequences of these criminal actions on victims. According to this research, victims experience trauma, self-blame, anxiety and worry about their future safety over a long period of time (Greenberg and Ruback, 1992). Unfortunately, criminological research has devoted much less attention to the aftermath of fraud victimization (Titus and Gover 2001:134).

A recent survey carried out by the National Victim Support Unit on victims of burglary list how the victims felt after a burglary:

	All	Male	Female
Angry	72%	72%	73%
Shocked	55%	50%	58%
Worried	43%	39%	46%
Fearful or scared	39%	28%	46%
Targeted	26%	31%	23%
Helpless	22%	23%	20%
Guilty or ashamed	7%	7%	7%
Fearful or afraid for children	13%	10%	15%

(www.victimsupport.org.uk)

Rape victims and those who suffer abuse in terms of domestic violence also have similar characteristic feelings following their abuse: 'The interconnections between victimization, other stressful life events, and mental health have a substantial research history. A wide range of consequences are associated with the experience of interpersonal violence in general, and sexual assault in particular, including depression, increased fears, sexual problems, anxiety, guilt, nightmares, sleep difficulties, nervousness, tendency to be re victimized, phobias, substance abuse, exaggerated startle response, and aggression' (Hlavka, Kruttschnitt and Carbone-López 2007: 896).

According to *Rape, its Emotional Consequences* by Schwartz, the feelings of shame and guilt are also emphasised, as is the lasting damage: 'It is always disturbing to me that those clients who have suffered the violent crime of rape feel ashamed and guilty. Despite all we know today about psychology, the psychology of rape, i.e. that it is not a sexual but a violent crime and the fact that women who have suffered this horrible fate were not at fault, so many of them persist, for years afterwards, in feeling guilty and ashamed of themselves. I guess that is the main point, that rape is a crime that damages the self-esteem and dignity of a person at the deepest levels' (Schwartz 2008:1).

VICTIM GROUPS OF OCCUPATIONAL FRAUD

There are many victim groups, discussed below, when unscrupulous employees steal from their employers. Such perpetrators act without emotion or empathy and often believe that they are entitled to the money or assets they are stealing. They do however leave a trail of destruction and hurt which goes well beyond financial loss. Many re-offend and go to jail, sometimes two or three times. They seemingly do not learn from their mistakes - how can they?

'Fraud effectively is what they do, and it becomes a primary or secondary profession. They have no respect for auditors, are often well-qualified accountants themselves' (Gill 2005).

'Because they have no conscience and lack any empathy for other human beings, they leave a trail of broken and psychologically damaged colleagues, managers, company owners and others in their wake' (Hare1993).

Croall has this to say on the subject of victims of occupational fraud, or as she describes it, occupational crime: 'Whether offenders are at the top or bottom in the hierarchy, it can be argued that their 'power' lies in the possession of knowledge based on their occupation and the trust which victims do not have... from a victim's perspective, the harm, rather than the status of the offender, is the key feature'. (Croall 2009)

GROUP A - THE VICTIMS OF SMALL
AND FAMILY-OWNED BUSINESSES

The researcher observed the following within the various companies and the victims interviewed. The obvious victims are firstly the company shareholders in the company where these criminals are employed. It is too easy to say victims lose only money. The company may for example be a family-owned business that is expected one day to be sold to enable the founder and major shareholder to have a comfortable retirement. In cases where the company fails due to the resultant cash-flow problems there are many more victims. The director shareholders would be the major ones. Their managers and staff, and the families of all these people, are all potential victims. All of them suffer one way or another. The workers and staff lose their jobs and often their pensions; the owners lose their investment and future income and also lose the respect of their work force. This is because often the employees blame the owners for having trusted the perpetrators.

B - LISTED COMPANY VICTIMS

Fundamentally, when considering employee fraud, there is little difference in the psychological damage caused to victim managers. This may surprise many people, as in most large public listed companies the managers and/or directors may not own shares in the business, and therefore do not lose money directly. They do however suffer the same psychological damage as the owner managers in much smaller companies. One might anticipate that because these victim managers are 'only employees' themselves they would not suffer in the same way. They do suffer, and often lose their jobs because of the fraud.

In many cases stress-related illness adds to the problem; the person concerned cannot easily find other work. To add to this psychological damage, it is often extremely hard for the victim manager to explain what has happened when applying for a new position. This is simply because large listed companies and financial institutions will not report the fraud, fearing bad publicity. Often, they also insist on the executive responsible for the fraud signing a compromise agreement before any payoff is sanctioned. The compromise agreement forbids the ex-employee from discussing in any detail the circumstances surrounding his dismissal.

Large financial institutions account for their financial loss in their bad debt reserve (Warrington

2007). This lack of reporting fraud to the authorities violates UK company law. There is a responsibility to report all fraud in a listed company. There is also the same requirement in some privately owned businesses. A privately owned business can be as small as the corner shop or very large, eg turnover in hundreds of millions. It is not necessary for a large operation to be listed on the stock market. The rules that apply state that if the company has any shareholders who own 26% or more in the business and are not active in the day-to-day operation, fraud must be reported (Companies House 2007).

C - SUFFERING OF VICTIMS AND COMPANIES

The companies and employees who are victims of fraud in terms of embezzlement also suffer at the hands of occupational fraudsters. To illustrate that there are many victims, Croall, quoting Levi, succinctly summarises this growing problem:

'Organisations are victims of embezzlement, employee theft and many other frauds and are particularly vulnerable to offences involving the financial or technical expertise of employees. While organisations may be seen as 'legitimate' targets, losses are passed on to consumers and workers. For example: In one victim survey, Levi (1995) reported that: Banks lost £3.2 million; clients or customers lost £1.8 million to 11 white-collar fraudsters; employers lost £1.7

million to 28 employees; suppliers of goods and services lost £1.1 million to 10 white-collar offenders and insurance companies lost £230,000 to 9 white-collar offenders' (Croall 2001a: 85).

Many victims suffer emotional and psychological damage that could remain with them the rest of their lives. Others develop stress-related illness. Such illness reported in the authors research includes latent heart problems such as fibrillation, angina, heart attacks, stress-related diabetes and some forms of cancer including breast cancer. The American Institute of Stress lists 68 illnesses that they believe can be triggered by stress (AIS 2008).

Death has been known to occur following the bullying carried out by fraudsters who manipulate co-workers and anyone that gets in their way. The size of a company has no relationship to the likelihood of its becoming a victim of occupational fraud. The only difference is in the amount stolen and what happens to the company following fraud. Quite often where the company is relatively small there is a cash-flow problem which eventually leads to the failure of the company. According to the British Chamber of Commerce report in 2004 'Setting Business Free from Crime', 'up to twenty percent of small/medium size companies fail due to the resultant negative cash-flow caused by fraud and stealing' (BCC 2004).

In the United States, The Association of Certified Fraud Examiners also states: '20% of business failures are as a direct result of employee fraud. The only other difference is the size of the fraud' (ACFE 2006).

With small companies, like a corner shop, a relatively small amount of money lost to a fraudster can causes the company to fail. This can be as low as £10,000, a large sum of money for a small business. Large multinational corporations can lose millions to sophisticated fraudsters and still survive. Martin Gill in *Learning from Fraudsters* interviewed sixteen fraudsters in jail; his rule for the investigation was that he would not interview those who had stolen less than £50,000. His chosen fraudsters to be interviewed had stolen between £60,000 and over £25million (Gill 2005).

D - OTHER VICTIMS

Families of fraudsters are also victims when a family member, a husband or a wife gets caught stealing from their employer. In many cases the spouse or partner had no idea that their loved one was stealing. They are shocked and in most cases they lose the respect and love for their partners and the relationship ends. If they are a married couple, divorce is often the end result. This is especially true where the fraudster is jailed. In family companies where fraudsters are apprehended, they invariably do not go to jail. The senior family member, often the founder and major shareholder, does not report to the authorities, seeing these decisions as protecting his family.

Sometimes the spouse or partner is aware, as they have helped hide the ill-gotten gains. In some cases, to protect themselves, the fraudsters use their wives' or husbands' bank accounts. This has the effect of ensuring that the partner does not talk, as they are by default implicated and could be seen in law as aiding and abetting a fraudster. In the author's research one case was investigated where the fraudster openly referred to his wife as his insurance policy.

Families of fraudsters suffer perhaps in a different way from managers working in victim companies, but there is no doubt that not only the partners but their children suffer. They suffer similar emotional and psychological harm, as do the families of victim managers. The suffering is not only financial. Indeed in many cases the psychological damage itself causes undue hardship and lasting scars. In some cases, especially where the partner and children had no idea about the activities of the fraudster, they end up moving to another area in the country in the hope that the shame does not follow them. Moves of this nature were observed in three of the companies investigated.

In many cases involving prosecution, victims of occupational fraud are treated only as witnesses. The courts and indeed some judges do not understand that the victims of such crimes will suffer. One prosecuting state attorney interviewed in the USA believes that in many of the cases he has prosecuted the judges were too lenient towards the perpetrators. Judges make comments such as 'no one was hurt' (Warrington 2007).

VICTIMS OF WHITE-COLLAR CRIME

Victims of white-collar crime suffer in the same tormented way as do victims of occupational fraud. They suffer trauma and psychological harm which in many cases stays with them for years and in some cases, be it financial or emotional, dramatically changes their lives.

Croall in *The Victims of White-Collar Crime* discusses conceptualising white-collar crime and corporate victimisation; it also covers what is known about crime and victimisation and discusses policy and support in relation to victimisation from corporate and white-collar crime. There are many misunderstandings with regard to the meaning of white-collar crime. Croall goes a long way to help define the term when associated with the wide range of offences committed by the 'powerful', be they wealthy individuals or corporations. Croall quotes from Slapper and Tombs (1999): 'Classic white-collar crime, which involves personal gain at the expense of employers, the government or clients (which can also be described as occupational fraud)'.. Offences, which involve increased profits or the survival of the organisation, often known as organisational or corporate crime' (Croall 2009:80).

Others prefer to use the broader term 'economic crime', which is used in many European countries, particularly in Scandinavia. Economic crime can be defined as 'crimes of profit which take place within the framework of commercial activity' (Korsell, 2002:201).

It can easily be seen from the above descriptions that it is not easy to decide, when a financial crime is committed, exactly how to categorise the offence. Many authors use the term 'white-collar crime' when, as in this research, a more specific definition may be more appropriate in categorising the offence (Croall 2009:80).

White-collar and corporate victimisation covers many crimes against consumers, ranging from investors and savers to pricing offences, food frauds and food safety. In fact she includes all the white-collar crimes committed by organisations as described by Sutherland, as well as modern crimes by mobile phone operators and cowboy builders.

Croall states: 'Those consumers are generally regarded as the main groups victimized by white-collar and corporate crime'. She also attests that all consumers are subject to fraud, safety and health threats and deception from the production and sale of consumer goods and services. Although these crimes are serious, many are not widely regarded as crime. 'While all consumers, irrespective of gender, age or social economic status, are affected, it can be argued that victimization reflects wider social inequalities' (Croall 2001b)

The 2009 web text 'Combating white-collar crime in Canada' by Michael Kempa from the Department of Criminology, University of Ottawa, covers many of the issues being faced in Canada by white-collar criminals. In his conclusions he states:

This report has highlighted some of the tremendous costs of, and driving factors behind, corporate and individual civil victims of white-collar crime. It has become clear that white-collar crime misappropriates massive financial resources, contributes to market instability and poor market performance and leads to all manner of secondary victimisation effects including psychological distress and stigmatisation (Kempa 2009:12)

White-collar crime and the victims of such crime are a complex and somewhat neglected subject. The relationship between victim and perpetrator can often be difficult to define. As an example, an employee in a senior position of trust could be just an employee, but is more likely over many years to have developed friendships with colleagues. This relationship can be either superficial or indeed a real friendship with the families of both parties socialising. This is where the employer's perception of an employee changes and the employee is in effect trusted more because of the friendship. When ultimately a fraudster is exposed who was a friend as well as a colleague, the feelings of betrayal become more severe and personal. Shapiro summarises this abuse of trust in *Collaring the Crime and Not the Criminal*:

The concept 'white-collar crime' therefore encompasses a spurious relationship between role-specific norms and the characteristics of those who typically occupy these roles. Corporate, occupational, and upper status is related to the distribution of positions of trust, which, in turn, provide opportunities for abuse. But that correlation does not justify skipping the intermediate step and identifying the abuses with the status of the perpetrators. Indeed, the correlation between corporate, occupational, or high status and abuse of trust is far from compelling. Offenders clothed in very different wardrobes lie, steal, falsify, fabricate, exaggerate, omit, deceive, dissemble, shirk, embezzle, misappropriate, self-deal and engage in corruption or incompetence by misusing their positions of trust. (Shapiro 1990:358).

The opportunity for fraud and abuse in a position of trust is enhanced when trust has become more personal. This is perhaps why most victims are initially in denial, because their own judgment of friends is in their minds questionable.

Babiak and Hare in *Snakes in Suits* discuss many cases of abuse by psychopaths in business. On the subject of victims, they elaborate on many of the feelings that victims suffer following the trust betrayal:

Emotional and psychological abuse is much harder to evaluate by outsiders, although it can be devastating to those in a psychopathic relationship. Emotional abuse often leads to anxiety, distress, depression, inability to sleep and generalized fear. Psychological abuse can lead to lowered self-esteem, feelings of unworthiness, self-doubt, and psychological pain. Individuals abused by psychopaths feel they are not themselves or something is wrong with them. They often blame themselves for the abuse, wondering, 'What did I do wrong?' Because our thoughts and feelings affect how we behave, victims may begin to do poorly in their jobs and get easily distracted, agitated, reticent, or overly emotional. Psychopaths use emotional and psychological abuse to control their victims. (Babiak and Hare 2006: 285).

Babiak and Hare devote a chapter to giving advice to victims of abuse and strongly recommend that victims seek professional advice in order to help recover from their feelings of guilt, trust betrayal and feeling foolish. They also talk about their anger and the need to get even with the perpetrator. 'By the time the victims contact us, they are in the stage where they feel intense anger towards the person who manipulated and abused them, and they want to get even. We believe that this may be a healthier stage to be in, as long as the victim does not act on these feelings' (Babiak and Hare 2006: 288).

John Clarke, a psychologist from Australia, also covers this subject in *Working With Monsters*. Clarke has done much research in the corporate arena on the subject of pyschopathy in the workplace. On the subject of psychopathic occupational fraudsters he states this about the victim:

Victims characteristically report feeling as though they have lost control over their lives. Panic attacks, depression, disturbed sleep and nightmares, relationship problems, confusion, disbelief, guilt, lack of trust, anger, powerlessness, flashbacks, shame, embarrassment and sexual dysfunction are just a few examples of how victims suffer. (Clarke, 2005:183)

Martha Stout in *The Sociopath Next Door* looks at the hurt caused by such criminals. Stout is a practising psychologist, who writes from the point of view of treating victims who have suffered at the hands of sociopaths. 'How can I tell who to trust?' it would appear is a question asked by many of her patients. Stout says: 'Since my patients are survivors of psychological trauma, most of whom have been devastated by other human beings, this is not a surprising concern for them to have' (Stout 2005: 9).

White-collar victims, along with victims of occupational fraud, often suffer self-doubt following the initial realisation that trust has been betrayed; the denial that someone or some organisation that they trusted with their money has let them down is hard to overcome. The aspect of being 'conned' and cheated by individuals that they had not only trusted but had worked and socialised with adds a further dimension that makes coming to terms with events very difficult. Victims cannot easily accept that they have been duped out of their hard-earned savings and/or investments by unscrupulous and extremely clever fraudsters. This self-doubt arising out of being taken in, coupled with anger, often leads to emotional and psychological disorders as well as stress-induced medical conditions. These conditions can be debilitating and add to the self-doubt, which in turn can lead to depression and nervous breakdown. In the relatively rare cases that go to court it is unfortunate that many court officials, including judges, only see the victims as witnesses. (Brock 2007)

EMOTIONAL AND PSYCHOLOGICAL
SUFFERING OF VICTIMS

This section discusses the emotional and psychological suffering of victims. Accidental discovery of fraud is a common theme. The denial after first discovery is seen with all victims. Other emotions suffered by victims include anger and the seemingly overwhelming initial need for revenge. Some managers of perpetrators blame themselves and consider that they have failed as managers because they did not know what was going on in their organisations. Some victims describe what they believe to be stress-induced medical conditions.

INITIAL FINDING

The authors' interviews with victims allowed various general conclusions relating to the method or means of discovery of the frauds. The most surprising conclusion was the fact that in all cases investigated, the fraud was discovered not by audit either internal or external, but predominantly by accident, someone in the company noticed something that was not quite right. If this person was in a less than senior position then it could be argued that this discovery was whistle-blowing, the senior staff then becoming involved. In companies where there was no internal audit team, senior management carried out the initial investigations followed by their auditors. It could be argued from the findings that there was always a chance discovery, if not by management then by the whistle-blower.

Dealing firstly with the only two institutions questioned which were very large, the means of discovery illustrates the above points. In the first organisation, the interview was carried out informally and not recorded. This was an extremely large government department whose internal auditors prefer to be known as counter-fraud teams. They indicated that their mode of operation was to carry out small divisional seminars which highlighted the problems of fraud. During these educational talks, employees are encouraged to make notes of odd behaviour and report them to the counter-fraud teams. This department relies heavily on employees to report any suspicion's of fraud or corruption. There is a special phone number for frauds to be reported and anonymity is ensured if the whistle-blower wishes. This mode of operation, it would appear, works reasonably well as it does discover many small frauds as well as some larger indiscretions. The organisation prosecutes practically all the discoveries, even for amounts as low as £1000. Whistle-blowing is therefore the main source of discovery and is encouraged.

The second very large organisation was an international bank with several divisions. They had internal audit teams who were usually brought in after something odd had been reported. The person from this bank agreed to be interviewed informally with no recording. From the interview it became apparent that this very senior manager had direct experience only in his division. He was heavily involved with the investigation of this fraud because he was held to be responsible, as it was his department where the fraud took place. A new recruit in this division reported that he had noticed in some of the files that he had been asked to review several names which rang bells. He had seen these names in a previous employment; they had been associated with fraud. The manager interviewee then called in his internal audit team. In both these organisations the frauds was really discovered by accident, although internal audit teams carried out the investigations. Accidental discovery featured high in the interviews.

DENIAL

Denial is the conscious refusal to perceive that painful facts exist. In denying latent feelings of homosexuality or hostility, or mental defects in one's child, an individual can escape intolerable thoughts, feelings, or events (Britannica Online 2008). An article in the *New York Times* summarises the problem of denial in the early paragraphs:

> Everyone is in denial about something; just try denying it and watch friends make a list. For Freud, denial was a defence against external realities that threaten the ego; today many psychologists would argue that it can be a protective defence in the face of unbearable news, like a diagnosis of cancer. In the modern vernacular, to say someone is 'in denial' is to deliver a savage combination punch: one shot to the belly for the cheating or drinking or bad behaviour, and another slap to the head for the cowardly self-deception of pretending it's not a problem.

> Yet recent studies from fields as diverse as anthropology and psychology suggest that the ability to look the other way, while potentially destructive, is also critically important to forming and nourishing close relationships. The psychological tricks that people use to ignore a festering problem in their own households are the same ones they need to live with everyday human dishonesty and betrayal, their own and others'. And it is these highly evolved abilities, research suggests, that provide the foundation for that most disarming of all human invitations, forgiveness.

> In this emerging view, social scientists see denial on a broader spectrum from benign inattention to passive acknowledgment to full-blown, wilful blindness on the part of couples, social groups and organizations, as well

as individuals. Seeing denial in this way, some scientists argue, helps clarify when it is wise to manage a difficult person or personal situation, and when it threatens to become a kind of infectious silent trance that can make hypocrites of otherwise forthright people. (Carey 2007)

This applies to an earlier case mentioned of a fraudster whose wife, the daughter of the owner, refused to accept that her husband had done anything wrong.

This prompted further research with the discovery of the term 'co-narcissism'. This term is applied to people who live with alcoholics or drug-addicted partners. The partners of NPDs are not only sympathetic to the plight of their loved ones but also think that in some way they are to blame. Alan Rappoport, a practising psychotherapist in California, introduced this term in his paper on 'Co-narcissism: how we accommodate to narcissistic parents'. Rappoport describes the term as follows: 'I have coined the term 'co-narcissism' for this adaptation, which has the same relation to narcissism as 'co-alcoholic' has to alcoholism and 'co-dependent' has to dependency. Co-alcoholics unconsciously collaborate with alcoholics, making excuses for them and not confronting them about their problem in an assertive way. The same is true of the co-dependent person, who makes excuses for the other's dependency and fills in for him or her as necessary'.

From the informal interview with this victim of occupational fraud it was apparent not only that his whole family were suffering but that he had no idea that their son-in-law had a personality problem. He did state that his daughter was always a caring person and worked hard to care for others.

Rappoport sums up this quality very well: 'People who behave co-narcissistically share a number of the following traits: they tend to have low self-esteem, work hard to please others, defer to others' opinions, focus on others' world views and are unaware of their own orientations, are often depressed or anxious, find it hard to know how they think and feel about a subject, doubt the validity of their own views and opinions (especially when these conflict with others' views), and take the blame for interpersonal problems'.

In many of the companies investigated it was apparent that the perpetrators never accepted blame for their actions, whereas in this company the daughter was to an extent shouldering the blame.

> Narcissistic people blame others for their own problems. They tend not to seek psychotherapy because they fear that the therapist will see them as deficient and therefore they are highly defensive in relation to therapists. They do not feel free or safe enough to examine their own behaviour, and typically avoid the psychotherapy situation. Co-narcissists, however, are ready to accept blame and responsibility for problems, and are much more likely than narcissists to seek help because they often consider themselves to be the ones who need fixing. (Rappoport 2005)

ENVY AND JEALOUSY

The issue of envy and jealousy also features in many of the companies investigated. This is a strong feature in the recorded interviews with several of the victims. Envy and jealousy are seen as the same thing by the layman; in examples from interviews what is really being cited is envy, the feeling that someone else is doing better. If we couple this feeling with the sense of entitlement, one of the characteristics of narcissism, we can observe two of the NPD characteristics listed in DSM-1V, characteristics 5 and 8.

5)   Has a sense of entitlement, ie unreasonable expectations of especially favourable treatment or automatic compliance with his or her expectations

8)   Is often envious of others or believes that others are envious of him or her. (DSM-1V)

This sense of entitlement is also one of the elements which, according to Comer in his book *Corporate Fraud,* are necessary for fraud to take place. We can see that there is a strong relationship between the behaviour characteristics and the feelings of fraudsters. Comer mentions that many fraudsters seem to have "A Moral justification coupled with a strong sense of Entitlement" Much is written about envy and jealousy philosophers. Below is a quote from an article in *Psychologist Today* defining envy and jealousy. Although the word 'jealousy' is used in some of the interview quotes, the researcher believes that envy was really being described.

ENVY VS. JEALOUSY

Long lumped together by ordinary folks and scholars alike, envy and jealousy are not a single, formless 'super emotion.' On the contrary, they are distinct, with different components, and are in fact elicited by completely different situations and in completely different settings. According to Georgetown University psychologist W. Gerrod Parrott, envy occurs when a person lacks another person's superior quality, achievement, or possession, and desires it - or wishes that the other person lacked it. Jealousy, by contrast, occurs in the context of a close relationship when a person fears losing an important other to a rival - in particular, losing a relationship that is important to one's sense of self.

For all their distinctiveness, envy and jealousy sometimes occur together', Parrott reports in the *Journal of Personality and Social Psychology* (Vol. 64, No. 4). "For instance, when a romantic partner gives attention to an attractive rival, a person may feel both jealous of that attention and envious of the rival for being so attractive. And since jealousy involves the loss of a personal relationship, it's usually more intense than envy".

Here's how envy and jealousy stack up:

Envy

- Feelings of inferiority
- Longing
- Resentment of circumstances
- Ill will towards envied person often accompanied by guilt about these feelings
- Motivation to improve
- Desire to possess the attractive rival's qualities
- Disapproval of feelings.

Jealousy

Fear of loss, suspicion or anger about betrayal. Low self-esteem and sadness over loss. Uncertainty and loneliness, fear of losing an important person to an attractive other, distrust. (*Psychology Today* 1994)

ANGER AND REVENGE

Initial feelings of anger at being taken in by trusted colleagues manifested itself in some cases investigated as an obsessive need for revenge. In one case the founder of the company and major shareholder admitted that he at times he became so angry that he felt like having his son-in-law harmed. In *Snakes in Suits* these feelings of anger are discussed:

UNFAIR TREATMENT

An interview with the commercial mortgage department manager of a major bank was of particular interest to the researcher, as it helped confirm what had previously been suspected. For some time in this research it had become apparent that by not reporting frauds to the authorities companies were breaking company rules in the UK. There is an obligation in listed companies to report all frauds. (Companies House ND). The researcher had confirmed from various sources the treatment of lost money in large organisations; it is put into bad debt reserves. Most financial institutions have a bad debt reserve, which can be as high as 15% of turnover. Commercial companies also have bad debt reserves on their balance sheets, but not as high a percentage as with banks. What had been puzzling the researcher was how large institutions got away with not reporting major frauds. The question was put to the interviewee of this bank. He laughed and said that as he was no longer employed by the bank he would explain. 'It's quite simple', he said, 'We had a board meeting and decided that we had made a bad investment in Mr X. Where do you put bad investments? In the bad debt reserve!'

In one company a senior staff member had died following years of bullying by the perpetrator. This case is interesting because apparently he died the day following the company's announcement that they were filing for administration. He had suffered a massive heart attack. This was following a serious cash flow problem brought about by the dishonesty of the company's FD. There are two important facts in this case: one, according to the researcher's interviewee, the employee's family were blaming the perpetrators' bullying for their loss. They also informed the interviewee that their brother had no history of heart problems and had never been to see his GP with heart related symptoms. Two, this manager's stress was apparently caused because he was almost 63 years of age and was looking forward to his retirement. He strongly believed that at his age he would not be able to find alternative employment.

Bullying is common in many of the companies interviewed. Because of this bullying there are staff casualties along the way. Some are more serious than others. Bullying and harassment not only has a negative effect on businesses and is unacceptable on moral grounds but is in breach of employment law in the UK. If management do not identify and deal with this problem they become vulnerable to prosecution by the victim. They may be taken to court or the industrial tribunal system by the victim (Business Link UK). The price of trust can therefore be high; in many cases the hurt is not only the money but the betrayal of trust. In most cases the perpetrators are employees who have risen through the ranks to senior positions and are totally trusted, not only with the companies' money, because of their position of responsibility.

While it cannot be proved beyond doubt that these stress-induced medical conditions and one death were caused by the trauma of fraud in these organisations, the fact remains that they are real. The author decided to look further into stress induced illness.

STRESS AND STRESS-INDUCED ILLNESS

According to the 'Healthy People 2000' report from the US Department of Health and Human Services: 'Stress has a great impact on our health. 70 to 80% of all visits to the doctor are related to stress and stress-induced illnesses. Stress contributes to 50% of all illness in the United States. The cost of job stress in the US is estimated at $200 billion annually including costs of up to absenteeism lost productivity and insurance claims.'

In the UK the Health and Safety Executive summarizes the following statistics on stress in the workplace:

'In 2007/08 an estimated 442,000 individuals in Britain who worked in the last year believed that they were experiencing work-related stress at a level that was making them ill, according to the Labour Force Survey (LFS). The 2007 Psychosocial Working Conditions (PWC) survey indicated that around 13.6% of all working individuals thought their job was very or extremely stressful. The annual incidence of work-related mental health problems in Britain in 2007, as estimated from the THOR surveillance schemes was approximately 5,750 new cases per year. However, this almost certainly underestimates the true incidence of these conditions in the British workforce.' (PCW 2007)

According to the American Institute of Stress there are no fewer than 68 medical conditions that may be triggered by stress. These include abnormal heartbeat (arrhythmia), angina pectoris, breast cancer, depression coronary thrombosis, diabetes high blood pressure other cancers and insomnia.

What reaction in the human body courses excess stress to trigger medical conditions? The Institute says:

Most of these effects are due to increased sympathetic nervous system activity and an outpouring of adrenaline, cortisol and other stress-related hormones. Certain types of chronic and more insidious stress due to loneliness, poverty, bereavement, depression and frustration due to discrimination are associated with impaired immune system resistance to viral linked disorders, ranging from the common cold and herpes to AIDS and cancer. Stress can have an effect on other hormones, brain neurotransmitters, additional small chemical messages (prostaglandins) as well as crucial enzyme systems and metabolic activities that are still unknown. Research in these areas may help to explain how stress can contribute to depression anxiety and its diverse effects on the gastrointestinal tract, skin and other organs. (www.stress.org).

STRESS AND THE IMMUNE SYSTEM

How can the body when reacting to stress and trauma cause medical conditions and illness?

'Stress also has a profound impact on the immune system, the network of organs, tissues and white blood cells that is responsible for defending the body against disease. The powerful stress hormones suppress the immune system making the body less capable of fighting disease and infection. Simply stated, stress suppresses the immune system's ability to produce and maintain lymphocytes (the white blood cells necessary for killing infection) and natural killer cells (the specialized cells that seek out and destroy foreign invaders), both crucial in the fight against disease and infection' (Hoeger, 2002).

Avoiding white-collar fraud

Is it possible for companies to avoid becoming the victims of occupational fraudsters? The author believes that by educating companies and making directors more aware of risks, it is, provided company directors become more alert to the possibilities. It need not be expensive to put in place simple anti-fraud policies.

In his research into the psychopathy of fraudsters and early warning signs, the author found that all companies investigated had basic anti-fraud policies in place; the problem was that these measures were not always monitored by management. As an illustration, the easiest anti-fraud policy to put in place is to have two signatures on all cheques. This could be modified to require only two signatures for amounts over a certain value, say £5000. While this procedure is easy to implement and many banks insist on it, to the determined fraudster it is open to abuse, particularly if the system is not monitored by management. In his research the author came across several cases where this anti-fraud measure was abused. In simple terms the fraudster would approach the co-signature person just as he/she was about to leave the office or go into a meeting saying 'could you please sign this cheque, I promised Mr X from company ABC I would get a payment in the post today.' Invariably the cheque would be blank. How many businessmen say 'never sign a blank cheque'? This happens more than you would expect, because fraudsters are usually senior and trusted staff members.

Having carried out the research the author believes that with the involvement of companies coupled with educating directors as to how fraud can be avoided, followed by the implementation of in-house solutions and protection methods, occupational fraud can be reduced. Of all the companies investigated not one, before discovering fraud in their organisation, even suspected that they could one day become a victim. Prevention is far preferable to dealing with fraud after it occurs.

ANTI-FRAUD POLICIES

This section will discuss some anti-fraud measures and other ways of preventing companies becoming vulnerable prior to hiring. Also discussed are corporate governance procedures such as matrix management, 360-degree evaluation and whistle-blowing procedures.

Occupational fraud has grown rapidly during the last decade. The poor economic climate since 2008 certainly has not helped. Research and many annual surveys on the subject show the phenomenon has been growing in monetary terms for decades.

In the ACFE Report to the Nations 2009, published in 2010, an estimated figure for the world economy shows a figure of $2.9 trillion lost from businesses worldwide. This equates to about $108 billion, or approximately £72 billion, lost to the 2009 UK economy by white-collar fraudsters (ACFE 2010).

Fewer than 50% of UK listed companies have effective anti-fraud measures in place (BDO 2005). The figure is undoubtedly considerably less in private companies; many small to medium-size UK companies cannot afford the staff overhead of initiating effective anti-fraud measures. More importantly, many do not even consider that there is a risk. Dr Paul Babiak asserts: 'Almost four out of 10 business owners in Britain view the possibility of fraud- particularly being ripped off by one of their own employees-as being the biggest threat to their company' (Babiak P 2006)

Occupational fraud is undoubtedly a major problem to UK businesses. Only a very small percentage of cases are reported and the financial losses are getting larger each year for reported incidents. This is also true in the United States. Babiak also claims that there is a bull market for occupational fraud in the United States.

'Organisations undergoing major changes such as downsizing or mergers provide a chaotic atmosphere that the savvy psychopath exploits. They cosy up to a firm's power brokers, manipulate co-workers and intimidate underlings on their way up the corporate ladder, stealing everything possible along the way.' (Babiak 2006)

Babiak also states that rich pickings are available to such industrial psychopaths, because of corporate mergers and acquisitions.

EARLY WARNING SIGNS

When occupational fraud is detected in companies, it is usually by accident; someone notices something odd and investigates. The Association of Certified Fraud Examiners believes that in the main frauds are discovered by whistle-blowing. The author's contention, from his research remains as stated above, by accident. This accidental discovery of an oddity or anomaly does then translate into whistle-blowing. Sometimes fraud is detected by internal audit. Many cases go undetected for years before the perpetrator finally gets caught. Usually because the fraudster makes a mistake, or simply becomes complacent thereby prompting an investigation. In most cases there are early warning signs that are not purposely ignored, simply not seen for what they may mean. This is because business owners and company directors are not, per say, on the lookout for occupational fraud, they trust their employees. As an example, an employee who repeatedly comes in early, leaves late and works some weekends and holidays for no apparent reason may be seen by management as being keen to please, a good employee. In reality he is merely using the additional time to carry out his fraud and attempting to cover his tracks by falsifying company records.

EARLY WARNING SIGNS - ACCOUNTANTS

Accountants and audit companies generally will define several telltale signs that could indicate that an employee may be less than trustworthy. The commonly accepted signs by accountants are as follows:

1) Arriving early, leaving late.
2) Working weekends and holidays for no apparent reason.
3) Not taking holidays.
4) Expensive cars for himself and family members.
5) Expensive holidays to exotic locations.
6) Moving into an expensive house or having a mini-mansion built.

TYPICAL COMPANY EARLY WARNING SIGNS:

1) Rising costs without explanation.
2) Unexplained margin erosion.

3) Unexplained or unexpected cash flow problems.

4) Suppliers insisting on dealing with one employee.

5) No audit checks on new employees.

6) Employees with external business interests.

7) Customer complaints, missing statements.

EARLY WARNING SIGNS - PSYCHOLOGISTS

Psychologists who have experience of occupational fraudsters may well add to the early warning signs listed by the accounting profession. Consider the following. An angry person, who is a compulsive liar and a bully, takes advantage of his/her position, is critical of other staff, bends the rules and does not conform. He or she would also be quick-tempered, exploitative and manipulative. Most employers would not suspect that an employee with the characteristics in the above sentences would pose a possible threat in terms of occupational fraud. Employers in general do not distrust their employees unless they have been given cause. Splitting out the characteristics and awarding marks in line with the key below could indicate a possible problem that would justify further investigation these questions should be addressed to a close work colleague and analysed by a professional with experience in the field of corporate criminality.

1) Is ———An angry person?

2) Is ———A compulsive or pathological liar?

3) Is ———The corporate bully?

4) Does ———Takes advantage of his/her position?

5) Is ——— critical of all other staff regardless of position in the hierarchy?

6) Does ———Bends the company rules?

7) Does ——- not conform?

8) Is ———Quick tempered?

9) Is ———Exploitative?

10) Is ———Manipulative at all levels?

Score as follows:

Characteristic never present - score 0.

Present some of the time - score 1.

Always present - score 2.

A score of ten or more would indicate the need to take a further professional look at the employee in question.

The ten questions above are taken from the author's 76 questions used in his research. The questions which were not in sequence but randomised were later analysed with an appropriate analysis spread sheet.

Of all the accountants interviewed either formally or in informal conversations only two and both Americans were prepared to give credence to the above test.

However Clarke in Working with Monsters suggests a similar approach:

'Following is an example of a questionnaire that can be given to as many people who know the job applicant as possible. The questionnaire is very similar to a traditional 360-degree review; however the questions are designed to specifically assess workplace psychopath and antisocial type behaviours in the organisational setting. Scores are tallied at the end. If the applicant scores within a certain pattern or range; scores, this suggests that additional investigation is necessary. Some sample questions from a total of ninety include:

1   Does ——— take responsibility for their behaviour?

2   Has ——— ever played one person against another in your office?

3   Has ——— ever had an affair to your knowledge with a person they work with?

4   Does ——— constantly look for new things to excite them?

5   Would you say that ——— has career aspirations that are realistic?

6   Has——— ever taken credit for work that you or someone else has done?

7   Has——— ever been on performance review or some other form of management plan?

8.   Is ——— prepared to do whatever it takes to get what they want, regardless of the cost to

10. Does ——— ever act without thinking about the consequences of their behaviour?

12. Does——— ever lose their temper for short periods of time to make people afraid of them?

13. Who do you think is the most important person in ———'s life?

'The rationale behind asking people other than the job applicant about previous performance is to get as balanced a view as possible. One drawback of using this questionnaire is that it is sometimes difficult to find previous colleagues who are willing to provide answers. This is not necessarily because the applicant: is a workplace psychopath. It may be that the applicant has not informed their employer they are applying for a new job, colleagues may be difficult to find or approach discreetly, and many colleagues simply do not have the time to complete the questionnaire. A good consultant who is experienced in the area should have developed appropriate systems to circumvent these problems'. (Working with Monsters P 239/240)

With a possible catalogue of early warning signs as detailed above it is hard to believe, but nevertheless true in many cases, that they are not recognised for what they could be by trusting managers. Are such fraudsters therefore extremely clever, or just lucky? Possibly neither applies. Management typically are not on the lookout for fraudsters in their organisations; they trust their employees. As an example, why would a top manager not trust a plausible chartered accountant who is not only in a responsible position but is trusted?

When considering all the facts it is not surprising therefore that few, less than 10% of occupational frauds are reported to the authorities. To illustrate the apathy that exists when considering reporting occupational fraud below is a quote from the 2004 Norwich Union Fraud Report.

'Most UK insurers (and many banks) no longer report the majority of frauds detected by them to the Police, due to the very low historic take up rates. For example, in 2004 Norwich Union detected approximately 4,000 frauds with evidence levels that they believed to satisfy the test of 'beyond all reasonable doubt' . Of these, only 41 were considered likely to be accepted by the Police on the basis of either:

a) significant public interest
b) involvement of organised crime, or
c) extraordinarily high levels of evidence.

Of these 41 'super frauds' submitted, 27 were investigated, with 18 coming to Court. All 18 prosecutions subsequently resulted in convictions. However more than half resulted in non-custodial sentences'. (NU 2004)

Not every company can afford to put in place an internal audit team but the author believes that to install several relatively simple procedures much headway can be made provided that management can be educated to realise that it could happen to them.

To introduce some or all of the procedures listed below and to ensure that they are monitored on a regular basis could help to prevent fraud.

Companies should introduce fraud policies such as:

1)   Split responsibilities, eg purchase ledger and sales ledger.

2)   No single person should collect, record, bank and reconcile cash or payments.

3)   Separate duties in purchasing process.

4)   Rotate staff and duties.

5)   Tighten procedures for authorizing expenditure.

6)   Random checks by management.

Research showed that in all companies investigated there were at least some of the above measures in place, but management never did any monitoring. In very large companies such as large internationals and banks with internal audit teams, it was only after someone in the organization noticed that something looked odd or did not add up that such teams became involved.

The author believes that prevention is better than cure and to this end he would recommend certain measures to be taken by companies at the recruitment stage to avoid making a mistake by hiring a potential fraudster. Such measures would be psychometric testing and handwriting analysis.

Dealing with handwriting analysis first, during his research the author obtained handwriting samples from five fraudsters who had been prosecuted, found guilty and jailed. These fraudsters had also been diagnosed by court-appointed psychologists and found to be suffering from personality disorders as in NPDs or industrial psychopaths. These samples were mixed with a further fifteen random handwriting samples. A senior member of the British Institute of Graphologists was asked to look at the samples and write a report on all of the twenty samples. The person in question is also a psychologist and past chairman of the Institute. All five of the convicted fraudsters were identified and characteristic traits identified from the handwriting, indicating the likely presence of a personality disorder.

A number of members of the BIG work for companies, attached to the Human Resources Department. These companies it would appear always insist in having applicants apply in the first instance with a handwritten application letter, while CVs may be typed. The members consulted by the author insist that following this initial screening and subsequent psychometric testing, their companies do not suffer from occupational fraud. Whether this is true in one hundred percent of their companies is irrelevant, as clearly this testing and screening will help in reducing the incidence of occupational fraud.

Below is a brief history of handwriting analysis taken from the BIG web site. This is followed by a discussion on psychometric profiling and testing.

HANDWRITING ANALYSIS

The science of interpreting handwriting has been studied and documented for some 3000 years. It originated about 1000 years BC in China. According to Dr Eric Singer: 'It has long been accepted by all societies that the signature of a man can be used to identify his transactions: this signature is now accepted by law, on bonds, deeds and other official documents. If you make an affidavit for a Court of Law, you confirm it with your signature. By writing your signature on a cheque you dispose of your own money. To forge another person's signature is a crime heavily punished by the criminal law of every country.'

We all recognize writing on envelopes from close friends and relatives and have noted that our own handwriting suffers when we are under emotional or physical stress. Therefore it is not surprising that efforts should be made to compare handwriting with emotions, with character and with strengths and weaknesses.

In 1875, the French Abbot Jean Hippolyte Michon coined the word 'graphology', from the Greek word meaning to write, 'logos' meaning 'doctrine' or 'theory'. Although the term 'graphology' is relatively recent, the subject itself dates back many centuries, having originally (as far as we can tell) been taken from southern India to China and from there to Greece, circa 2,000 BC.

Coming closer to the present day, relatively

speaking, Aristotle wrote: 'Just as all men do not have the same speech sounds, neither do they all have the same writing', and Confucius is recorded as having observed, 'Handwriting can infallibly show whether it comes from a person who is noble-minded or from one who is vulgar'. But it was not until 1622 that the study of handwriting was put into print, by the Italian Camillo Baldi, in 'How to recognize from a letter the nature and quality of a writer'. This was little more than a collection of random observations though, and remained virtually unnoticed.

At the beginning of the 19th century, the German Lavater and two Frenchmen, Edouard Hocquart and Abbé Flandrin, developed the art of interpreting handwriting. But it was not until the second half of the century, when Michon published the results of his many years research into individual handwriting movements, that the subject began to arouse public interest. His method gained popularity owing to its simplicity; he studied certain elements in handwriting, namely the 'stroke', the 'letters', the 'words', the 'baseline', 'paragraphs', 'free movements' ('i' dots and 't' bars), 'flourishes', 'punctuation' and 'paragraphs'.

However, Michon's method of allocating one specific movement to represent one aspect of character, and in particular his assertion that the lack of a movement indicated the opposite characteristic, is now recognized as only being partly accurate. Michon's successors, particularly his student, Jule Crépieux-

Jamin, disagreed with this principle, and also with the practice of attributing rigid interpretations to single signs. Crépieux-Jamin, who spent his life collating and improving upon Michon's observations, is today credited with founding the Société Francais de Graphologie. He defined the various elements of handwriting which today form the basis of the French school of graphology, and divided these elements into seven categories: Dimension, Form, Pressure, Speed, Direction, Layout and Continuity.

To every element in the handwriting, Crépieux-Jamin attributed a range of possible meanings; he insisted that the value of any given sign is not fixed and that its significance and interpretation can vary depending upon the other features in the writing. This theory is now supported by all professional graphologists. In other words, no single feature in handwriting can be taken reliably to represent anything about the writer, unless it is supported by other factors in the writing.

At approximately the same time in Germany, William T Preyer recognized the fact that 'handwriting' is in fact 'brainwriting'. He correctly postulated that should the writer lose his writing arm, as did Nelson for example, and have to use the opposite hand, or even the mouth or foot as in the case of paralysis, the same basic tendencies will appear in the script, although obviously not executed with such fluency at first.

In 1897, the 2nd Graphological Periodical was

founded in Germany by Hans Busse (who also formed the Association for Graphological Research). The chief contributors were Dr Georg Meyer and Busse's assistant editor, Dr Ludvig Klages. Meyer's work was important, but even his greatest contributions were overshadowed by the eminence of Klages. Later, Klages moved to Switzerland, where he was to continue his research work and create the first complete and systematic theory of graphology. Also in Switzerland, Dr Max Pulver, a renowned psychologist who had a deep interest in graphology, was to make a further contribution in terms of the symbolism in handwriting, both in direction and in symbolism of space. His division of the handwriting into the three vertical 'zones' explains aspects of the handwriting previously misunderstood, with his formulation of the 'Three Dimensions' - vertical movement, horizontal movement, and depth - providing an integral understanding of graphology as we know it today.

These latter graphologists, Preyer, Klages and Pulver, made greater attempts than their predecessors to appreciate the inner psychological causes of graphic expression. They were able to draw upon a more highly-developed understanding of a psychological characterology which for the first time attempted to penetrate the psyche of the writer.

Many books began to appear as the subject gained public interest, some of whose authors also furthered the science of graphology, including Robert Saudek, a

Czech graphologist who came to live in England, who is acknowledged as having established 'speed' in handwriting. Today, no serious graphologist would consider assessing handwriting without first ascertaining the speed.

Hans Jacoby, a contemporary of Saudek's, also produced books aimed at the general public, based upon what he termed 'the science of the expression of movements', revealing that gestures seen in the writer's body language, ie manner of walking, expressive movements of hands and arms, etc, were also reflected in the handwriting.

Alfred O. Mendel's book *Personality in Handwriting* included a lengthy dissertation on pressure in handwriting, in which he introduced a new approach to the interpretation given to direction of pressure, depending upon the writer's personal proclivities, and demonstrated that this single subject could be broken down into many different areas, each of which indicated highly-revealing aspects of the writer.

Klara Roman, a Hungarian graphologist who emigrated to the USA, included the results of considerable research into pressure in her excellent book *Handwriting, A Key To Personality*, (recently reprinted by the Institute). And in Germany, Professor Rudolph Pophal (whose books are currently being translated into English) who held the Chair in Psychology and Graphology at the University of Hamburg, brought graphology into the area of research and made many discoveries related to brain and muscle structuring. These confirmed the earlier assertion of Preyer's that handwriting is indeed 'brain writing'.

GRAPHOLOGY COMES TO BRITAIN

Although fairly well established on the European continent, notably Germany and France, graphology was largely unknown in this country until the Second World War. At that time, many graphologists, amongst them Dr Eric Singer (a student of Klages), came to Britain, hoping to continue their profession in a country where the subject was virtually unknown. In order to bring it to the attention of the public, several graphologists began producing popular books for 'the man in the street', including *Graphology For Everyman* (now available in the trilogy of Singer's books, *A Manual of Graphology*). This was a breakthrough in the subject, with public reaction indicating the demand for more information on the subject.

In 1982 the Graphology Society was formed by Patricia Marne, a journalist and author of several graphological books, and her colleague John Beck. The Graphology Society offered the first meeting place with regular lectures for anyone interested in the subject. The following year, Francis T Hilliger, a student of Dr Singer's, founded The British Institute of Graphologists, which was constitutionally formed with elected committee, regular meetings and a quarterly journal,

The Graphologist. Frank Hilliger devised a system of graphology which further simplified the process of analysing handwriting, reducing the number of categories within signs, based upon a method for establishing the speed and form level of the writing. His system was much less complicated and therefore easier to learn, proving so successful that upon setting up the Institute the Hilliger system was adopted for the examination syllabus. (The British Institute of Graphologist, 2009)

PSYCHOMETRICS

Like handwriting analysis, it is believed psychometric assessment was used in China as long ago as 2000 BC. The emperors apparently used very extensive written examinations to assess and select officials for government departments. The word 'psychometric' is derived from the Greek words for measurement and mental. Such tests are used extensively in business today as part of recruitment selection procedures. Psychometric tests attempt to assess your mental ability and suitability for a particular position, and also your personality. Occupational psychometric tests are designed to provide employers, particularly in large organisations, with a reliable way of selecting the most suitable applicants for jobs or for promotion.

Psychometric tests are seldom used in isolation and represent just one of the methods used by employers in the selection process. The usual procedures for selecting candidates still apply, for example: A job is advertised and you are invited to send in your CV, which is then checked to see if the organisation thinks your experience and qualifications are suitable. It is only after this initial screening that you may be asked to sit a psychometric test. These tests aim to measure attributes like intelligence, aptitude and personality, providing a potential employer with an insight into how well you work with other people, how well you handle stress and whether you will be able to cope with the intellectual demands of the job.

PSYCHOMETRIC TESTING IN PRACTICE

There are two main types of psychometric test, ability tests and personality assessment tests. Ability tests look at your ability to carry out different tasks. This gives the company performing these tests an idea as to whether you have the right level of ability to fit in with their requirements. Part of ability testing is to look at logical reasoning and also to try to establish how you think, and thus your aptitude for the vacancy offered. Such tests are usually multiple-choice questions and have a time limit. Personality assessment tests are also usually multiple-choice tests and may start with a profile of the type of person the company envisages filling their vacancy. Personality questions try to establish how you would fit in with other members of staff. More and more companies today are using psychometric testing, either in house, or, particularly with smaller companies, by outside testing centres. The Psychometric Success Company briefly describes the type of company using psychometric testing: 'Psychometric testing is now used by over 80% of the Fortune 500 companies in the USA and by over 75% of the Times Top 100 companies in the UK. Tests are used by many employers across most sectors, including IT, engineering, energy, banking, consultancy, accountancy, the civil service and other public sector, fast-moving consumer goods and retail' (Psychometric Success 2011).

The author has personal experience of using psychometric testing in business and found the tests extremely useful and reliable. He did however discover within his own organisation some twelve years ago a weakness, though this was not in any way a criticism of the testing itself. One departmental manager was refusing to act on the results. Invariably he would overrule test results in the mistaken belief that candidates in his opinion 'would be OK once employed'. The author, who was the company's chairman at the time, discovered several examples where new employees did not live up to expectations and were eventually dismissed. After several incidents with this department he decided to investigate himself, in an attempt to find out why the testing had apparently let his company down. When he read the personnel files of the recently-dismissed employees he discovered that the psychometric test had clearly indicated lack of suitability for these positions. The department manager concerned admitted that the tests had shown these candidates should not have been employed; he pleaded, in mitigation, pressure from his boss to fill the vacancies. It must be stressed however that this was the only department in the organisation to have overruled the psychometric testing. The company continued to use the tests after tightening up its internal controls on recruitment and usage of psychometric testing. The department manager concerned was also given additional training on the use of psychometric testing. The company had no further problems.

Modern psychometric testing is relatively speaking a new phenomenon, and psychologists who specialise in this form of psychology can be extremely well qualified with experience that merits extremely high salaries and benefits.

Below is a brief history of modern psychometric testing taken from the Psychology Majors website. This is part of an introduction for the benefit of psychology graduates who may be thinking of taking up psychometrics as a career:

THE HISTORY OF PSYCHOMETRICS: THE STUDY OF THE HUMAN MIND

In psychology history (psychology is, of course, the study of the human mind) there hasn't always been an emphasis on rigorous assessment and evaluation. After all, psychology is, typically, about the inner workings of the mind of the individual and how it impacts life and behaviour. The desire to not just study the inner working of the mind but to actually measure things like function and intelligence gave rise to the branch of psychology known as psychometrics.

Psychometrics is a popular psychology specialty, and has become a popular focus for psychology students at the graduate level. Psychometricians are in high demand, and are needed in both the public and private sectors.'

HISTORY OF PSYCHOMETRICS

In 1879, Sir Francis Galton published an article in which he described an experiment in 'mental operations'. The experiment he conducted would later be called 'free association', where he assessed reaction to a list of 75 words. According to a paper by Larry Ludlow of Boston College, he threw his resulting thoughts into a 'common statistical hotch-potch' and determined (a) the rate at which ideas were formed (50 per minute), (b) the frequency of recurrent associations (about one half), (c) the frequency within periods of his life that associations could be attributed (showing 'in a measurable degree, the large effect of early education in fixing our associations'), and (d) the character of associations that occurred (verbal, sensory, 'histrionic').

The impact of this first venture into psychometrics is still relevant today. Thirty years later, Charles Spearman took Galton's idea to the next level. He developed the idea of measuring human intelligence while studying with Wilhelm Wundt, the founding father of a different branch of psychology known as psychophysics. L L Thurstone, a contemporary of Charles Spearman, developed the idea of comparative judgment (a theoretical approach to measurement). Alfred Binet of France became the first psychologist to apply psychometrics when he was asked to create an intelligence test that would evaluate children (this led to the Binet Scale).

The work of all of these men contributed to the emerging field of psychometrics and planted the seeds that would eventually grow into more specific intelligence testing, personality testing and vocational testing, as well as many other areas of psychological measurement.

(Psychometric Majors 2011)

Clarke, in his book *Working with Monsters*, adds this cautionary note on psychometric testing:

> 'Organisations that use psychometric testing often assume that psychopathy will be detected. This is a dangerous assumption to make, as the majority of psychometric tests used do not directly screen for psychopathy, they are generally personality and IQ tests. These types of personality tests are relatively easy for the psychopath to fake' (Clarke, J 2005).

MATRIX MANAGEMENT, 360-DEGREE
EVALUATION AND WHISTLE-BLOWING

Some large companies try to implement not only sophisticated anti-fraud measures and policies but other tools designed to encourage detection and in particular whistle-blowing. Such measures would also include 360-degree evaluation, anonymous reporting of colleagues and managers and matrix management.

360-degree evaluation is simply where employees are encouraged on a regular basis, say annually, to evaluate their co-workers and their managers.

Anonymous reporting is in some organisations used extensively as the main weapon against employee fraud. This method is in fact encouraging whistle-blowing.

Matrix management is used in many multinational organisations almost as a necessity. Put simply, employees have to report to more than one boss but in different areas of expertise. This is usually where large projects are undertaken on a global basis. These projects are typically managed by a person with the required qualifications and expertise. He will naturally have a line manager in headquarters. He will also have to report to the manager in the country where he is managing the project. Because of the nature of what he is managing, he will also probably have to report to a finance manager. If he is working on a technical project, then his personal expertise may not include finance. He may also have somewhere a divisional manager.

The difference between matrix management and conventional functional management is in the number of 'bosses'. In the normal hierarchy of business, functional management is where each employee reports to only one supervisor or manager. The divisions in companies would typically be sales, marketing, engineering, finance, product development etc.

Project organisation is where the team has many levels of expertise and therefore has cross-functional expertise. Matrix management therefore combines both conventional functional management and project-oriented management. One company that used all of the above methods was Enron (McLean and Elkind 2004). None of these procedures however stopped the massive corporate fraud within the Enron Corporation.

WHISTLE-BLOWING

In the context of this work, whistle-blowing is informing management and/or a company's auditors about wrongdoings in a company or organisation. This would mean informing management about the whistle-blower's suspicions with regard to a colleague or other staff member in the organisation. In the ACFE 2009 Report, whistle-blowing is referred to as an anonymous tip, in many cases through a purposely set up hotline. The following extract from the ACFE report illustrates well the topic of whistle-blowing:

'While tips have consistently been the most common

way to detect fraud, the impact of tips is, if anything, understated by the fact that so many organizations fail to implement fraud reporting systems. Such systems enable employees to anonymously report fraud or misconduct by phone or through a web-based portal. The ability to report fraud anonymously is key, because employees often fear making reports due to the threat of retaliation from superiors or negative reactions from their peers. Also, most third-party hotline systems offer programs to raise awareness about how to report misconduct. Consequently, one would expect that the presence of a fraud hotline would enhance fraud detection efforts and foster more tips. This turns out to be true. The presence of fraud hotlines correlated with an increase in the number of cases detected by a tip. In organizations that had hotlines, 47% of frauds were detected by tips, while in organizations without hotlines, only 34% of cases were detected by tips. This is important, because tips have repeatedly been shown to be the most effective way to catch fraud. The better an organization is at collecting and responding to fraud tips, the better it should be at detecting fraud and limiting losses. In 67% of the cases where there was an anonymous tip, it was reported through an organization's fraud hotline. This strongly suggests that hotlines are an effective way to encourage tips from employees who might otherwise not report misconduct. Perhaps most important, organizations that had fraud hotlines suffered much smaller fraud losses than those without. Those organizations also tended to detect frauds seven months earlier than their counterparts'. (ACFE2010 Global Fraud Study)

The author in his research did not cover whistle-blowing, because in most cases investigated fraud was discovered by accident; someone in the company noticed something that was not right, or didn't look right. It is true to say that following the accidental discovery, the employee who found the anomaly by accident, then reported the facts to management, became a whistle-blower. None of the companies investigated had in place an anonymous hotline set up to encourage whistle-blowing. The author was however aware in one large organisation researched that there was an informal policy to encourage whistle-blowing, but it had little success in that most frauds discovered by this method were relatively small offences but nevertheless were fraud. These would include dishonest expense claims and overtime claimed when not worked.

ACFE FRAUD PREVENTION CHECK-UP

What else can be done to avoid occupational fraud? The Association of Fraud Examiners has produced an excellent paper on fraud prevention, available on a DVD by request or the entire document can be downloaded in PDF format. The opening statement in this document states: 'One of the ACFE's most valuable fraud prevention resources, the ACFE Fraud

Prevention Check-Up, is a simple yet powerful test of your company's fraud health. Test fraud prevention processes designed to help you identify major gaps and fix them before it is too late.'

The document goes on to describe the benefits for companies in taking this test:

Since fraud can be a catastrophic risk, taking the ACFE Fraud Prevention Check-Up can save your company from disaster. If you do not proactively identify and manage your fraud risks, they could put you out of business almost overnight. Even if you survive a major fraud, it can damage your reputation so badly that you can no longer succeed independently. The ACFE Fraud Prevention Check-Up can pinpoint opportunities to save you money. Fraud is an expensive drain on a company's financial resources. In today's globally competitive environment, no one can afford to throw away the five percent of revenues that represents the largely hidden cost of fraud. Those businesses that have identified their most significant fraud costs (such as insurance and credit card companies) have made great strides in attacking and reducing those costs. If your organization is not identifying and tackling its fraud costs, it is vulnerable to competitors who lower their costs by doing so.

Fraud is a common risk that should not be ignored. Fraud is now so common that its occurrence is no longer remarkable, only its scale. Any organization that fails to protect itself appropriately faces increased vulnerability to fraud. It is the least expensive way to find out your company's vulnerability to fraud.

Most organizations score very poorly in initial fraud prevention check-ups because they don't have appropriate anti-fraud controls in place. By finding this out early, they have a chance to fix the problem before becoming a victim of a major fraud. It's like finding out you have seriously high blood pressure. It may be bad news, but not finding out can be a lot worse.

It is a great opportunity for your organization to establish a relationship with a Certified Fraud Examiner (CFE) you can call on when fraud questions arise. CFEs are experts in detecting fraud and helping organizations prevent it in the future.

Strong fraud prevention processes help increase the confidence investors, regulators, audit committee members and the general public have in the integrity of your company's financial reports. This could help to attract and retain capital.

(ACFE Fraud Prevention Check-Up 2011)

METHODS USED BY FRAUDSTERS

In his research the author identified many and varied methods used by occupational fraudsters to steal from their company. The following list is not an exhaustive list but covers the methods identified positively during the research. The list serves to illustrate the more common methods discussed with victim companies. Fraudsters appear always to be looking for and implementing new and innovative methods. Many of the methods listed have several variations, but there would appear to be nothing completely original and new, merely variations on themes.

EXPENSES FIDDLES, SUBMITTING TRAVEL AND SUBSISTENCE EXPENSES NOT SPENT.

A classic for executives who travel extensively, is to fly coach but charge the company for first-class travel. The same goes for hotels and meals; fake invoices are manufactured and submitted. Fake taxi receipts are also a common fiddle observed in various companies.

DIRECT PAYMENTS

Stupid as this may sound, it is a very common method for fraudsters to use. Again because they are in a position of trust, the fraudster simply writes a cheque made out to himself or a family member. They sign it if they are authorised, or get a signature by deception. This is typically done using a ploy such as approaching the counter-signatory as he/she is leaving the office and saying: 'Can you sign these cheques? I promised I would get payments out today'.

A comment such as the quote above has been made in several of the companies interviewed. The requirement in companies for double signatures on all cheques is in fact a basic anti-fraud measure. The fraudster, to conceal the loss, alters the company books.

FAKE INVOICES

This is a classic way for fraudsters to cheat. Put simply, a fake invoice for a product or service is raised by an employee who is in a position of trust. He then authorises the payment himself. Sometimes, if he has the authority, he also writes the cheque. He may be able to sign the cheque too, but if a counter signature is required the cheque gets signed because the employee is in a position of trust. The fraudster may well have set up his own company in the name of the provider of product or services. There are many variations on this theme that have been tried and proven to work. Many accounting companies and auditors often refer to this fiddle as 'the classic case'.

FAKE EMPLOYEES AND LEAVERS LEFT ON PAYROLL

This form of stealing, because of its nature, requires that the perpetrator be in a position of power and trust; he/she must also have the payroll under their control. A variation on this theme is to continue to accrue for and subsequently pay to themselves commission still being accrued for a salesperson who has left the company.

GHOST EMPLOYEES

A variation on the above. Employee names are added to payrolls when they do not exist, and the salary payments find their way into the fraudster's bank account. This is a method commonly used where companies employ lots of temporary staff or casual workers.

CREDIT NOTES

Credit notes due to suppliers or customers are converted to cheque payments and various ways found to make sure that the credit is paid into the fraudster's bank.

OVERPAYMENTS BY CUSTOMERS NOT CREDITED

This method is not as common as some of the methods above. An overpayment or a duplicate payment made in error by a customer or client is put in a suspense account. After a period of time, typically well over a year, if the customer has not made a case for a refund, a cheque is raised and finds its way into the fraudster's bank.

DUPLICATE PAYMENTS

Duplicate cheques are raised for a supplier or customer; one finds its way into our perpetrator's hands.

COMPANY CREDIT CARDS

Charging personal items to a company credit card is, surprisingly, not always picked up by auditors. The person concerned is usually in a position of trust and can easily charge the items to various journals that are legitimate for his/her company.

PRIVATE CAR EXPENSES

Items in this category usually end up being charged against another employee's company car.

Deposits and payments for private cars, household items and holidays

Another common variation; charges may be made direct by cheque or again on the company's credit card.

FORGING SIGNATURES

The simple act of imitating a co-worker's signature is seen by some perpetrators of fraud as an easy way to obtain cash. In many cases they are caught, because they simply carry out a forgery with little attempt to copy the original. Research found no cases where banks had alerted the company. In some case investigated forged signatures were used internally on authorisation documents as a prerequisite to carrying out fraud.

In one case researched, the forged signature was not even a close resemblance of the original and had been used on scores of cheques. When the bank in question was asked why it had not alerted the company, it admitted that it did not really check signatures. There is no doubt that this company in particular had a strong case for compensation against their banker, as the sum stolen by this method was several hundred thousand dollars.

A staff member at the bank also alerted the perpetrator that she was being investigated before she was formally suspended and arrested. The outcome of this case was jail for the fraudster and no lawsuit against the bank. The company's lawyers strongly advised against pursuing a large bank.

Research has determined that occupational fraudsters are extremely innovative. Many variations on the above basic methods seen above have also been identified.

ACCOUNTING SYSTEM MANIPULATION

In addition to the well-used methods employee fraudsters use, there are also many innovative methods involving manipulation of computerised accounting systems. Managers of victim companies have explained the manipulation of accounting systems to cover fraudster's tracks detailed below. Occupational fraudsters are more frequently using computer technology to hide their crimes by falsifying company records. Internal fraudsters today are more computer literate than in the past and many are extremely skilled at manipulating systems to cover their tracks.

The traditional belief that accounting systems are foolproof is not entirely valid today. Data can nearly always be resurrected with the appropriate software, even after hard drives have been reformatted. Users outside the IT industry are not generally aware of these techniques, nor are most occupational fraudsters. To a great extent accountants and business managers rely on the premise that data cannot be erased because of the archiving principle. Accountants rely on this and take comfort from the belief that accidentally-erased data can always be resurrected from archives. This is not always true if a clever fraudster finds a way of manipulating an accounting system.

Resurrecting from archive does in fact work in some cases, as the following example illustrates. The company was a chain of restaurants; the group accountant had keys and unlimited access to all the restaurants in the chain. His mode of operation was to visit each restaurant during the night and change the records of cash takings. He reduced or erased entries showing significant cash receipts. This fraudster was caught because the owner of the business happened to know that a particular restaurant had taken a large amount of cash on a particular evening, yet this was not confirmed by bank statements. The group accountant was responsible for all banking, had been with the company for many years and was trusted. The owner brought in the authorities. The police forensic team resurrected all the entries from archive computer files and the perpetrator was prosecuted and went to jail.

The accepted principle of regular backup tapes is also a procedure intended to ensure integrity of data following system crashes and other unforeseen computer glitches. The grandfather-father-son system is used extensively in business. This system takes three numbered backup tapes on a daily basis. If five days' backups were deemed necessary then there would be 15 tapes, etc. One is stored in the accounts department, one in a safe on site and the third off site, just in case of fire.

Two examples illustrate that the determined fraudster can use the backup procedures for his or her advantage. A relatively small local charity, company C, had employed a female bookkeeper for many years. She became ill and died. Another female accountant was hired because of her computing skills on top of her accounting knowledge. The first thing she did was to convince management that all the accounting should be computerised; only payroll was. The trustees agreed and the accountant installed Sage, a well-known and respected accounting software package. She also convinced management that a daily backup should be taken and kept off site, at her home. This single backup was saved on a CD ROM. The accountant was a computer expert and contrived that the system crashed on a regular monthly basis. She was always on hand to restore the system, using, of course, her backup disc.

She was found to be on the fiddle when a supplier informed management that he had been paid twice for a particular invoice, but the company name was slightly different on one cheque.

This is of course the classic way corporate fraudsters operate, reference duplicate payments in the section of fraudster's methods. Cheques with false but similar names end up in fraudsters' bank accounts. This perpetrator made a mistake; she mailed both cheques at different times to the legitimate supplier. The police were brought in and the accountant was investigated. She had a duplicate accounting system in her home and had on a regular basis backed up the system with a fictitious disk. You cannot audit what is not there. After the court case it was revealed that she had been in jail some years earlier for occupational fraud using similar methods. The other company was in another town 150 miles away. As a further point of interest, the bug that was put on the system causing it to crash continued after she was arrested, and the charity eventually had to rebuild their system from scratch using outside experts who had failed to locate and neutralise the bug.

The second example was similar. In this case the finance director of Company D had been with the company for many years and had computerised all the accounting when the company was relatively small. When eventually found out, this perpetrator was using many and varied methods for stealing and had been taking company funds for about twelve years. Again he was discovered by chance; the chief executive noticed an oddity on the monthly management accounts and started asking questions. The finance director was suspended pending investigation. His office was searched and two unnumbered backup tapes were discovered. This company used the conventional system and had 15 legitimate numbered tapes. Again, resurrecting after a crash with false backup data made it impossible to satisfactorily audit the company's accounts. This firm too had regular system crashes, but in this example they stopped after the accountant's suspension.

The final example of a trusted employee manipulating an accounting package is far more elaborate and again was discovered by chance. The owner of the company asked a part-time accountant (the full-time chief financial officer was away on holiday) for the date when he had last paid a relatively small supplier. The accountant very quickly went back to the owner with the answer, but asked the owner to take a look at the computer screen. The date was there, but the entry showed zero in the amount field, it also showed zero (0.00) for the period. The owner quite rightly asked the accountant to bring the records back from archive. This highlighted an extremely elaborate scheme. There was no archive for this supplier. Impossible - or was it?

Many hours of discussion and investigations took place in the company, as of course everyone believed that what they were seeing was impossible. Eventually the accounting system software supplier was contacted, and he asked for various records in order that they could analyse the data and solve the problem. It appears that the chief financial officer had first used a little-used feature on this accounting package which made it possible for entries to be consigned to archive after each transaction or for each period. He had then used a systems analyst programmer friend and fellow employee to write a patch for the software, intended to erase the archive for the specific journal. Again you cannot audit what is not there. The supplier chosen for this scam was a little used one and had only had about £5000 through the account in six or seven years, not likely to be one chosen by auditors as a sample. The company never discovered the amounts siphoned from the company using this method.

The company dismissed the chief financial officer after they found other fiddles. The total amount found and proven quickly in order to discipline the employee was relatively small in comparison to the company turnover. The company therefore decided not to prosecute. The management of this company had reason to suspect that the programmer was blackmailing the fraudster. They discovered, through the grapevine, that their ex-employee had joined a much larger company as Finance Director. A year or so after he joined he was fired for stealing, and again not prosecuted.

The examples described are used as illustrations and are taken from interviews with managers of victim companies of occupational fraud. There are many more examples and opportunities for ambitious employees wishing to steal and cover their tracks if, as well as being accounting system aware, they also have a good grasp of computer technology.

Fraud reports

This chapter takes a look at some of the fraud reports which are published either annually or bi-annually, both in the UK and the United States. Initially quotations are from reports read by the author at the start of his research. Finally the most recent reports are discussed. The reader will clearly see from the recent reports how the costs to the economy have grown over this relatively short period of time.

FINANCIAL COSTS TO THE UK ECONOMY

According to the Association of Certified Fraud Examiners UK division, £200m a day is lost to the UK economy through economic crime. This figure was arrived at by dividing its estimated £72 billion per annum cost to the UK economy (*Observer* 2005). Put into perspective, this means that all economic fraud, including occupational fraud or employee fraud is costing UK businesses around £137,000 per minute.

Martin Gill estimates the cost to UK listed companies to be up to £2 billion annually (Gill 2004). On the other hand, the British Chamber of Commerce estimates the cost of crime against business, not necessarily listed companies, to be £19 billion a year. This survey is interesting in that it had a positive response from 46 of the total of 61 chambers in the UK. In total 2788 surveys were completed. This survey, while not strictly speaking relevant in its entirety to occupational fraud, does make some interesting observations:

a) 64% of businesses surveyed had experienced at least one crime within the last twelve months, an increase of 6% since the last crime survey conducted in 2001.

b) Furthermore, 47%, almost one half of businesses, had experienced more than one crime in the last 12 months.

c) Over half the businesses surveyed did not report all of the crimes committed to the police, and 16% did not report crimes at all. Nearly one third (32%) of businesses failing to report crime did so because they had no confidence in the police response (BCC 2004).

The growth in white-collar crime has escalated in the last decade. Babiak claims that there is a bull market for occupational fraud in the United States:

'Organisations undergoing major changes such as

downsizing or mergers provide a chaotic atmosphere that the savvy psychopath exploits. They cosy up to a firm's power brokers, manipulate co-workers and intimidate underlings on their way up the corporate ladder, stealing everything possible along the way' (Babiak2006).

Babiak states that rich pickings are available to such criminals, industrial psychopaths, because of corporate mergers and acquisitions. Conversely, Hare' his co-author on *Snakes in Suits*, prefers to categorise white-collared fraudsters as sub-criminals (Babiak and Hare 2006).

Both Hare and Babiak are convinced that many of the perpetrators of such crimes are psychopaths. The popular image of a psychopath is of a criminal committing violent crimes such as serial rape and murder. However this deviates quite markedly from reality. In contrast to populist notions, many crimes committed by psychopaths are unlikely to be violent; rather they are more likely to be implicated in cases of corporate fraud. Hare contends that psychopaths in business take advantage of co-workers by manipulation, bullying and compulsive lying to attain their goals (Hare 1993).

Listed companies only account for about 0.13% of UK registered companies. There are approximately two million companies registered in the UK. Of this number there are 1234 listed on the stock exchange and a further 1348 listed on AIM, Alternative Investment Market. The two million also includes very small one-man convenience companies (Companies House 2007).

Various estimates from organisations conducting surveys into occupational fraud suggest fewer than 10% of all corporate employee frauds are reported to the authorities, even fewer by financial institutions. One potential explanation for the financial institutions' reluctance to report victimisation is their aversion to bad publicity. It becomes more desirable to take care of the problem internally by offsetting the losses against bad debt reserves and simply firing the perpetrator.

Many financial institutions, banks and credit card companies in the US have reserves as much as 15% of turnover, a balance sheet item quoted as bad debt provision. According to one US state attorney interviewed, this is where many internal frauds losses are posted. It is easy to understand therefore the very large estimates attributable to all economic crime. (Brock 2007)

In public listed companies in the UK, there is a legal obligation to report financial irregularities, but in many cases ways are found to avoid the decision, usually because bad publicity is seen as a failure on the part of the Board. In private companies without outside shareholders there is no legal requirement to report. If however, the business ownership includes a non-active shareholder with 26% or more of the issued share capital, there is an obligation to report fraud (Companies House 2007).

SERIOUS FRAUD OFFICE ANNUAL REPORT

During 2005-06, the SFO began with 68 active cases involving an estimated £2.06 billion 'at risk'. This figure includes amounts judged to have been intended as well as actually obtained: the latter data are not separated out and published. The SFO is a reactive organisation which, deterrence and incapacitation notwithstanding, is not set up to play a preventative role, so its costs in anticipation and prevention are zero. Its estimated resource costs (expenditure) for 2005-06 were £41 million, which excludes costs incurred by the police and other investigators working on SFO cases. Confiscation orders made (but not necessarily paid) totalled £14 million, but an unpublished proportion of that would go to compensate victims in those cases. (ACPO 2007)

When analysing the detail behind these four fraud surveys, it is easy to understand why there are several estimates as to the size of the fraud problem and its cost to the UK economy. When considering the subject of the author's research, occupational fraud, and the various reports suggesting a very low reporting rate, it is understandable that estimates in this area are inconsistent. The Association of Certified Fraud examiners, in its 2006 fraud report in the United States, draws attention to this difficulty: 'At the outset, it should be clear to anyone who has spent time dealing with the subject of occupational fraud that attempts to accurately measure the frequency or cost associated with occupational fraud in the United States will be, at best, incomplete.'

This 2006 fraud report echoes the same conclusion on estimates as in the 2004 fraud report. The report further concludes that businesses, even after detection cannot be sure of the amount stolen:

'Fraud, by its nature, is hidden, and so the true amount of fraud taking place in U.S. businesses at any one time cannot really be known. Even attempts to measure the amount of fraud that has already been detected will lead to incomplete results.' (ACFE 2006)

SUMMARY OF RECENT (2010) FRAUD SURVEYS

Many accounting firms internationally and in the UK regularly carry out and publish fraud reports. The parameters used vary from company to company, for example some only look at prosecuted fraud while others look at frauds over certain thresholds, and this could be as low as £10,000 or as high as £100,000. Perhaps the best known and most respected fraud report is carried out by the Association of Certified Fraud Examiners in the United States. The ACFE 2009 report, published in 2010 for the first time, went worldwide. The association were then able to give a reasonable estimate as to the cost to the worldwide economy; this estimate is 5% of the Gross World Product. The Association of Certified Fraud Examiners stresses that this is an estimate.

We asked each CFE who participated in our survey to provide his or her best estimate of the percentage of annual revenues that the typical organization loses to fraud in a given year. The median response was that the average organization annually loses 5% of its revenues to fraud. Applying this percentage to the 2009 estimated Gross World Product of $58.07 trillion would result in a projected total global fraud loss of more than $2.9 trillion.

Readers should note that this estimate is based solely on the opinions of 1,843 anti-fraud experts, rather than any specific data or factual observations; accordingly, it should not be interpreted as a literal representation of the worldwide cost of occupational fraud. However, because there is no way to precisely calculate the size of global fraud losses, the best estimate of anti-fraud professionals with a frontline view of the problem may be as reliable a measure as we are able to make. In any event, it is undeniable that the overall cost of occupational fraud is immense, certainly costing organizations hundreds of billions or trillions of dollars each year.' (ACFE 2010).

If we apply the ACFE estimate of 5% to the UK Gross Domestic Product for 2009 expressed in dollars, the loss to the UK economy was $108.5 billion. Some of the UK companies investigated by the author also had losses to occupational fraud approximating to 5% of turnover. When analysing and applying this 5% in this analysis the author was ignoring fraud in larger organisations investigated, where the fraudsters embezzled many millions of pounds. These organisations lost very large numbers in real terms to occupational fraud, but their turnover figures were so large that expressing the loss as a percentage would be irrelevant.

Below are excerpts from this ACFE report and also from several fraud reports from UK companies and organisations.

ACFE 2010 REPORT TO THE NATIONS

Asset misappropriation schemes were the most common form of fraud in our study by a wide margin, representing 90% of cases — though they were also the least costly, causing a median loss of $135,000. Financial statement fraud schemes were on the opposite end of the spectrum in both regards: these cases made up less than 5% of the frauds in our study, but caused a median loss of more than $4 million, by far the most costly category. Corruption schemes fell in the middle, comprising just under one-third of cases and causing a median loss of $250,000.

The report emphasises that frauds are detected mostly by whistle-blowing or a tip-off. In the author's investigations he expresses this as 'by accident'. The accidental stumbling on things which do not look right prompts further investigation which then turns into so called whistle-blowing. The author stresses however that he only came across two organisations which had in place whistle-blowing facilities with anonymous reporting. 'Occupational frauds are much more likely to be detected by tip than by any other means. This finding has been consistent since 2002 when we began tracking data on fraud detection methods' (ACFE 2010).

The Association also discusses the effect on companies by size, which bears out the author's findings in his investigations: 'Small organizations are disproportionately victimized by occupational fraud. These organizations are typically lacking in anti-fraud controls compared to their larger counterparts, which makes them particularly vulnerable to fraud' (ACFE 2010).

When considering anti-fraud measures in the investigated companies, many had in place some, albeit simple, anti-fraud measures in place. The biggest problem discovered from interviews was that none of the anti-fraud measures in place were monitored, making them useless. The simplest one, often imposed by the company's bank, was the requirement for two signatures on cheques. This in some cases was modified to require two signatures on all cheques over a limit, for example £5000. The reason this procedure was abused was simply that the MD, who was usually the second signature, fully trusted his finance or accounting person. 'Anti-fraud controls appear to help reduce the cost and duration of occupational fraud schemes. We looked at the effect of 15 common controls on the median loss and duration of the frauds. Victim organizations that had these controls in place had significantly lower losses and time-to-detection than organizations without the controls' (ACFE 2010).

In the author's investigated companies, 85 percent of frauds were carried out by senior managers or directors. In several cases it transpired that the fraud had been taking place over several years. In one case the forensic accountants only went back ten years and found the perpetrator had expanded his take and had become more innovative with his schemes over the years. This particular fraudster was found out because he became greedier and caused the company in question cash flow problems. He was actually discovered when a senior executive probed into unexplained margin and profit erosion.

High-level perpetrators cause the greatest damage to their organizations. Frauds committed by owners/executives were more than three times as costly as frauds committed by managers, and more than nine times as costly as employee frauds. Executive-level frauds also took much longer to detect.

More than 80% of the frauds in our study were committed by individuals in one of six departments: accounting, operations, sales, executive/upper management, customer service or purchasing. More than 85% of fraudsters in our study had never been previously charged or convicted for a fraud-related offense. This finding is consistent with our prior studies. Fraud perpetrators often display warning signs that they are engaging in illicit activity. The most common behavioural red flags displayed by the perpetrators in our study were living beyond their means (43% of cases) and experiencing financial difficulties (36% of cases). (ACFE 2010).

The ACFE has in this 2010 report made great strides in estimating the costs of Occupational fraud, other companies also show figures which are estimates, who really knows the cost?

One of the American companies investigated by the author kept in touch. After their perpetrator was jailed, the accounts department was finding other examples where cash had been stolen, in some cases amounting to tens of thousands of dollars. These findings went on for at least three years. This company also found out, after the court case, that the perpetrator had been in jail previously for the same offence in a different state.

'Measuring the cost of occupational fraud is an important, yet incredibly challenging, endeavour. Arguably, the true cost is incalculable. The inherently clandestine nature of fraud means that many cases will never be revealed, and, of those that are, the full amount of losses might not be uncovered, quantified or reported. Consequently, any measurement of occupational fraud costs will be, at best, an estimate. Nonetheless, determining such an approximation is critical to illustrate the pandemic and destructive nature of white-collar crime'. (ACFE 2010)

KPMG 2009 FRAUD REPORT

This KPMG report begins by drawing attention to the increases in corporate fraud due to the economic downturn:

> Amidst the current economic downturn, and the pledges of renewed vigour of regulatory enforcement, our 2008–2009 Fraud Survey reveals serious challenges confronted by leaders in the public and private sectors. Since the latest economic downturn began, vast sums of market capitalization have been wiped out. Trillions more have been committed to stabilizing financial institutions, injecting liquidity into the capital markets and jump-starting the economy through infrastructure spending programs. The aftermath of the downturn has further uncovered numerous Ponzi schemes that caused investors to watch billions more vanish. (KPMG 2009)

It is interesting to note that a high percentage of executives interviewed by KPMG cite fraud as a significant threat in their industry. This finding is certainly at odds with the author's research findings. Only twenty percent of companies interviewed after frauds had been detected indicated that they had been aware of the possibility of fraud in their companies.

The ones who were aware of the threat also fell into the category of not monitoring adequately the anti-fraud measures in place within their organisation. The

KPMG report does however have a more international aspect:

> The majority of executives cite fraud and misconduct as posing significant risks to their industry today. Nearly two-thirds of executives (65 percent) reported that fraud and misconduct is a significant risk for their industry. If such wrongdoing were to be experienced, the greatest concern for over two-thirds of executives (71 percent) is the potential for a loss of public trust when market confidence is at a premium. (KPMG 2009)

KPMG certainly endorses the author's findings with regard to inadequate internal controls and monitored anti-fraud measures:

'Inadequate internal controls or compliance programs heighten the risks of fraud and misconduct. Two thirds of executives (66 percent) reported that inadequate internal controls or compliance programs at their organizations enable fraud and misconduct to go unchecked'. (KPMG 2009)

KPMG in this report highlight the effects of the economic climate and the opportunity for fraudsters, and go on to highlight areas which should be 'red flagged' within organisations:

> Experience suggests that periods of economic downturn can bring about elevated conditions for fraud and misconduct. Typically referred to as a 'fraud triangle',

these conditions include pressures, opportunities, and rationalizations for committing fraud. In the current environment, these increased risks may manifest themselves in the financial statement in multiple ways. Examples of red flags that gate keepers may wish to consider include:

- Revenue recognition. It is helpful if corporate overseers understand how sale transactions can be manipulated. When is a sale a temporary revenue-generating sleight-of-hand that will come back for credit? Credit memos can provide indications of abuse. Credit memo activity reviews should occur throughout the year, and it may help to graph them to look for patterns. 'Bill and hold' transactions have very specific tests that need to be met in order to record revenue. Specific controls and monitoring should be in place to ensure appropriate timing of revenue recognition. Large or unusual transactions near the end of a quarter should be flagged for specific review to be sure that revenue recognition criteria is met.

- Loan Covenants. The pressure becomes obvious when operating results or key ratios approach loan covenant thresholds. Corporate gatekeepers should pay close attention to financial data that affects covenants, and monitor when corporate loans come due for renewal. What are the covenants? What are potential trouble spots? What reported numbers are most sensitive to change and how can they impact covenants? What situations can lead to financial manipulation?

- Liability Accruals. There have been situations where companies have earnings per share above market expectations, but choose to report lower earnings per share to match competitors. This allows the company to establish a rainy-day reserve. Audit committees may wish to inquire about unusual or unexpected changes in operating results, liabilities, or subjective contra accounts (i.e., positive or negative). An added proactive step is to ask for after-the-fact monitoring reports to establish if management's estimates are reasonable.

• Subjectivity in the Balance Sheet. To understand how susceptible data is to manipulation, directors should consider drilling down on subjective balance sheet accounts and their underlying assumptions and key drivers. Corporate overseers may wish to monitor valuation allowances, assumed rates of returns on pension assets, processes to value illiquid assets, contingency accruals, and environmental reserves. It is often helpful to think about these account movements in subjective areas in the context of what it takes to move earnings per share.' (KPMG 2009)

Enablers of fraud and misconduct

Management's efforts to prevent, detect, and respond to fraud must be informed not only by its prevalence and nature, but also by the root causes of such misconduct. As such, we asked executives what factors may allow instances of fraud and misconduct to occur within their organizations. The most commonly cited were inadequate internal controls or compliance programs. Similarly, almost half of executives surveyed cited management override of controls, inadequate director oversight over management, and collusion between employees and third parties. A lower number of respondents, almost a third, cited collusion between management and third parties or between employees and management'. (KPMG 2009)

Price Waterhouse Coopers (Global Economic Crime Survey 2011)

FRAUD IS ON THE RISE

What about fraud more broadly? Two years ago, almost half of our respondents thought fraud was on the rise. They told us there were more opportunities to commit fraud, and more pressure to do so. They were right: our 2011 survey shows that more organisations are saying they have been victims of fraud. And this year's respondents think the trend is going to continue.

Economic crime does not discriminate. It is truly global. No industry or organisation is immune. We have seen a 13% rise since our last survey and organisations see more fraud ahead. The fallout isn't just the direct costs: economic crime can seriously damage brands or tarnish a reputation, leading organisations to lose market share. As society becomes less tolerant of unethical behaviour, businesses need to make sure they are building – and keeping – public trust. Our sixth Global Economic Crime Survey turns the spotlight on the growing threat of cybercrime. Today, most people and businesses rely on the internet and other technologies. As a result, they are potentially opening themselves up to attacks from criminals anywhere in the world. Against a backdrop of data losses and theft, computer viruses and hacking, our survey looks at the significance and impact of this new type of economic crime and how it affects businesses worldwide.

1. Know who you are dealing with among staff, suppliers, partners and agents.

2. Align IT, Internal Audit and the Board in the fight against economic crime.

3. Conduct regular fraud risk assessments.

4. Leadership by a cyber-savvy CEO, who instils a cyber risk-aware culture.

5. Implement a cyber crisis response plan.

In our survey, cybercrime ranks as one of the top four economic crimes. In our previous economic crime surveys, when we asked respondents if they had experienced cybercrime, the response levels were very low and statistically insignificant. As a result, we combined the results with 'other types of fraud'. We focused on cybercrime this year and reintroduced it in the 'types of fraud' question, asking respondents if they had experienced cybercrime in the last 12 months. Of those respondents who said they had experienced some form of economic crime, almost 1 in 4 said they had suffered one or more cybercrime incidents in the last 12 months (see figure 1).

So how and why has cybercrime emerged as one of the top types of fraud? We believe that:

• Because of media attention around recent cybercrime cases, organisations are more aware of this type of fraud and might have put extra controls in place to detect and report it.

- Because there is ambiguity around the definition of cybercrime and what it constitutes, respondents might have re-classified some of the more traditional economic crimes as cybercrime because someone used a computer, electronic devices or the internet to carry them out.

- Regulators are focusing on it more.

- Advancements in technology make it easier to commit cybercrimes. Also, almost half (48%) of those who had experienced economic crime in the last 12 months said they perceive the risk of cybercrime to be on the rise. Only 4% perceive the risk to be falling and the rest think it will stay the same. These statistics clearly show that cybercrime is a growing threat.

We studied the attractions of cybercrime compared with other conventional crimes. Cybercrime presents different risks and rewards to those conventional crimes. Take, for example, a cybercrime where an 'outside' fraudster infiltrates a banking system remotely to steal money or personal information. There are fewer risks when compared with physically stealing assets from an organisation:

- The fraudster is not present at the location in person, so there is less chance of getting caught in the act.

- There is less chance of law enforcement being able to identify the perpetrator or find out where they were based when they committed the crime. More often than not, the perpetrator is located in a different jurisdiction. This makes it harder to identify, arrest and prosecute them by traditional means. Current laws are not mature enough to prosecute cyber criminals with any impact. Technological advancements are fast-paced, which means the development of cybercrime is too. Organisations need to be up to date on the latest legislation and corporate policies to make sure they keep up.

- Given all these obstacles, the perpetrator can carry on returning to the scene of the crime with minimal fear of being caught. Organisations can put preventative measures in place to reduce the risk of traditional economic crimes like asset misappropriation, accounting fraud, or bribery and corruption, but with cybercrime, it's much harder. (GECS 2011)

The author did not look at cybercrime in his research but did in certain cases look in depth at some clever attempts by fraudsters to use technology to cover their tracks. The GCS Survey conclusions below will certainly give most business directors and owners food for thought:

Our survey results show that fraud is persistent, and that organisations need to be vigilant and proactive when fighting economic crime. 'Traditional' frauds like asset misappropriation, accounting fraud and bribery and corruption remain the top three that our respondents fell victim to in the last 12 months. But new' types of fraud are emerging – cybercrime in particular. With new ways of doing business, new technologies and changing work environments, come new risks and new ways for fraudsters to carry out crimes. Organisations need to be aware of these changes and adapt their response mechanisms and detection methods accordingly. This is even more true when it comes to new technologies. Smart phones and tablet devices, social media and cloud computing all offer a wealth of attractive business solutions and opportunities, but they can also be a Pandora's Box of risks and dangers.

Having a smart phone or a tablet device means carrying around your organisation's sensitive and confidential data in your pocket which without precautions in place, anyone might be able to access sensitive and confidential information and cause considerable harm, both financial and collateral. A decade on and the fraud risk continues to rise. Despite the effectiveness of risk management systems being deployed, there are always individuals or groups of individuals who are able to spot an opportunity and circumvent or override controls. This is especially true when it comes to cyber security. As headcounts fall in control functions across the globe, we fear more fraud will go undetected. Advances in technology are fast-paced, as are fraudsters, however organisations are often far behind. It is now essential to ensure that cyber and information security issues have the standing they warrant on an organisation's risk register. Those organisations ready to understand and embrace the risks and opportunities of the cyber world, will be the ones to gain competitive advantage in today's technology driven environment. Establishing the right 'tone at the top' is key in the fight against economic crime'. (GECS 2011).

Conclusions

GENERAL

The conclusions from the author's research are more far-reaching and disturbing than had been envisaged at the start of the investigations. Initially it was felt that the financial losses incurred, particularly in the small to medium business class, would have been the hardest issue for victims to come to terms with. This hypothesis is not correct. The lasting psychological damage and hurt felt by victims occurred in all companies investigated, regardless of size. Fraud leaves many scars and lasting debilitating psychological problems and in some cases stress-induced illness. The experience of the financial losses and the betrayal of trust, it would appear, leaves a lasting scar. The feelings of victim owners, founders, directors and managers, as well as shareholders, ranged from extreme feelings of anger and the need for revenge to a very deep feeling of being betrayed by trusted employees. The anger also appears to stay with victims, but the initial need for revenge wanes over a relatively short period. The victims know in their heart of hearts there is no way that revenge can be initiated without them, the victims, becoming criminals

Occupational fraud is far more widespread than had been thought prior to this investigation. No company is immune, that is to say, examples have been found in many and varied organisations. These range from the very small company with less than ten employees to multinational corporations employing hundreds of thousands of employees. Occupational fraud can take place in any organisation regardless of size and the numbers of staff employed.

An example, the manager of a department where fraud occurred, the mortgage department of a large international banking organisation, was blamed by the board simply because he managed the fraudster, even though he had not hired him. The manager was fired unfairly, and he and his family suffered as a direct result of the fraud. This manager, after losing his job, became depressed and suffered from stress; ultimately he had a nervous breakdown. He had worked for the bank for almost thirty years.

BUSINESS FAILURE AND ITS VICTIMS

One company not included in the original research, because the owner at the time refused to be interviewed, was contacted recently. Company K and its founder owner is a sad case of an occupational fraud victim. It has many of the ingredients discussed in this research (See Company K). The owner of the business was in effect conned, and he believed lies and deception with devastating results. Above all he was a victim of trust betrayal and paid the ultimate price of trust.

The founder believes that he was taken in by lies and deceit. During the telephone conversation he kept repeating, 'I trusted him with my money and my retirement'. He now considers himself a failure and to some degree he is still in denial. During interview he repeatedly commented that he still found it all hard to believe, even though his auditors had shown him much proof.

This successful businessman will take his guilt and shame with him to his grave. His feelings of shame come from the fact that his company had to file for administration, the ultimate failure for a businessman. His sin was trust.

A recent further meeting, after about eighteen months, with the victim banker of Company J also illustrates the feelings of failure. He is now some two months into his new venture. He started a small restaurant business without any prior experience. His intentions now are to build up the business prior to his retirement in about ten years. He is still very bitter and talks about wanting revenge, not so much on the perpetrator, but on his boss and friend who dismissed him because the board had to be seen to act and blame someone. His compromise agreement when leaving the bank made it virtually impossible to obtain employment commensurate with his banking experience. The ex-banker repeatedly expressed feelings of having been cheated out of his career as a banker. He now also believes that because he had not spotted the fraudster himself he is somehow to blame, and therefore a failure as a banker. He further commented that several times each day he still relives the events that caused his perceived failure.

FAILURE TO REPORT FRAUD

One common element became apparent in the early stages of the research; victim companies and their managers did not wish to be formally interviewed. The reluctance to discuss their experience was in most cases because of the perceived failure on the part of the organisation and the managers for not having seen what was happening in the area of their responsibility. In many cases, even where many millions had been taken, there was reluctance on the part of the board of directors to report the fraud to the authorities. The large financial organisation investigated did not report a loss running into millions. They used the bad debt reserve to account for the loss and convinced the board that they had made a bad investment.

An interview with a state attorney, a specialist in economic crime, confirmed that in the US financial institutions lose fraud losses in their bad debt reserves. He further indicated from his experience that the reserve on balance sheets can amount to 15% of turnover. This fact is a major concern, because in the UK, under company law, there is a legal obligation to report fraud whether occupational or other frauds associated with companies (Companies House 2007).

The reluctance of identified victims to discuss their experience on a formal basis is partly due to them not having reported their loss to the authorities. They strongly believe that the bad publicity following reporting the crime would have an adverse effect on the business. This reluctance is also due to embarrassment at having been taken in by a trusted employee. These facts made the research more difficult than was originally envisaged. In some cases many months went by with regular follow-up calls before a formal interview was granted. In several cases, after agreement had been reached, excuses were found not to go ahead. Following on from this reluctance and the victim's feeling of shame at being taken in by trusted employees, the effect of victim blaming in white-collar crime needs to be considered.

The concept of victim facilitation in major scams is quite apparent, because many scam operators convince their victims of benefits that can be made by agreeing to their proposal. In occupational fraud it could be argued that there is an element of victim facilitation. Put simply, this is because the victims of occupational fraud facilitate the fraud by trusting the perpetrator. Victims often blame themselves for not having noticed events which, with hindsight, became obvious. Titus and Gover discuss the aspect of victim blaming and compare white-collar crime victims with rape victims:

'Due to the influence of victim facilitation in many types of personal fraud, victim-blaming is common. Fraud victims often tend not to report fraud victimization due to the public's and criminal justice system's attitudes towards victims' culpability in the act (Walsh and Schram, 1980). For example, attitudes towards fraud victims have been compared to attitudes towards rape victims in that the victim has contributed to the incident. Some blame rape victims for contributing to the event by engaging in enticing behaviour or violating rules for preventive behaviour. This analogy has been made to fraud victims who entice fraudulent behaviour through greed or by failing to take appropriate precautions against the tactics of fraud perpetrators.' (Titus and Gover ND)

Occupational fraud victims, like rape victims, seem to be reluctant to report the crime to the authorities. Whilst company managers and directors resist informing the authorities because of the perceived bad publicity harming their companies, the individuals themselves fear any reprisals and blame. This largely applies to managers and directors who were the perpetrator's immediate manager.

REOFFENDING

Of further interest in this research was the discovery of the high rate of reoffending among these perpetrators. Without exception, in all cases where the perpetrator was prosecuted and subsequently jailed he had offended and been jailed previously.

The large financial institution partially investigated knew for sure that their fraudster had previously offended. It was the recognition of his name by a new recruit in his department that alerted management, who then called in the internal auditors. About a year after this fraudster had been fired without prosecution his ex-manager had a call from another organisation informing him that the perpetrator had reoffended. Once again, because of the fear of bad publicity, the perpetrator was not prosecuted.

In 80 per cent of the investigated companies there was evidence of re-offending. In some cases there was evidence given by interviewees that their perpetrators had continued to offend following dismissal and becoming re-employed. In other companies there was a strong suspicion that their fraudsters had offended before. Usually this information came to light following or during the investigations. One of the two companies with no firm verifiable evidence of previous or subsequent offences commented that they had strong suspicions of previous offending. This was based on the lack of satisfactory explanations regarding the fraudster's departure from three previous companies. Hindsight of course, but in this case, the pizza franchise in the US, the offender was the owner's son-in-law.

The question as to why these fraudsters re-offend cannot really be answered from this research. The suggestion would be that the extreme arrogance and sense of entitlement displayed by perpetrators exhibiting behavioural patterns of personality disorders is at least a factor. In a sense it is their profession; it is what they do, and they are professional fraudsters.

Another reason perpetrators re-offend is because they steal out of an economic need. Such a need was feeding a gambling addiction in the transport business investigated, Company B. Another perpetrator in Company I was believed by his management to be feeding a drug addiction.

TREATMENT FOR PERSONALITY DISORDERS

Looking at the concept of treatment for persons 'suffering from' or shall we say exhibiting characteristic traits indicating personality disorders. it is worth quoting from research into the treatment of psychopaths and other personality disorders including anti-social behaviour. Jessica H Lee, in *The Treatment of Psychopathic and Anti-Social Personality Disorders*, makes reference to a five-year study conducted by Black (1982), which study looks at psychopaths who have undergone treatment and their predisposition to reoffend following discharge from Broadmoor Hospital:

> It was discovered that the best predictors of low rates of recidivism were having fewer previous psychiatric admissions and fewer previous criminal convictions, while being classed as a psychopath was a positive determinant of re-conviction. In his review of studies of discharged special hospital patients, Murray (1989) also identified younger age, shorter length of stay in hospital and absolute, as opposed to conditional discharge, as correlates of subsequent re-offending. Like Black, he also discovered that re-offending is more likely to occur among those diagnosed with psychopathic disorder. (Lee 1999)

Lee's findings are certainly more scientific than the present research but the conclusions are similar: psychopaths re-offend.

SUMMARY

The emotional and psychological suffering of victims of white-collar crime, and in particular occupational fraud, can be far reaching and deep. From the initial discovery of the fraud, when victims are at best in denial, through to the eventual realisation that they had been taken in by employees that they had trusted, they can and do in many cases suffer lasting trauma.

In many of the cases investigated the initial denial manifested itself in a profound disbelief that fraud could have taken place. Some interviewees initially believed that it was all a mistake and would eventually be proven to be incompetence on the part of the fraudster. Eventually, when the truth was exposed, in some cases by internal audit and in others by external audit, the denial changed to an extreme feeling that trust had been betrayed. This betrayal of trust was hard for the victims to come to terms with. The reason was that the fraudsters had been known to the victims for many years in the working environment and with many, the perpetrators had become personal friends as well as colleagues. The victims had socialised with the perpetrators, had played golf together and in some cases had shared family holidays. The initial feelings that trust had been betrayed transformed in the early stages into extreme anger and the need for revenge. As time went by and victims received damning information from the forensic accountants, feelings of shame appeared, with the victims blaming themselves for not having realised what was happening in their organisation.

The concept of blame is also a two-edged sword, as in some companies the manager who supervised the fraudster was blamed by his own management. This blame could be described as part of the 'blame culture' which seems to be prevalent and growing in Britain. Blame culture is defined as 'a set of attitudes, for example, within a business or organization, characterized by an unwillingness to take risks or accept responsibility for mistakes because of a fear of criticism or prosecution' (BNET Business directory 2010).

In some of the smaller companies interviewed where the resultant negative cash flow caused the demise of the company, rank and file staff blamed the owner of the business for allowing the perpetrator to get away with the fraud. The strong feelings of staff who lost their jobs when the company they worked for failed, or was bought from the administrator, were understandable, because in these companies, in the main family owned, offenders were not prosecuted. In these cases the ex-employees and their families became victims through no fault of their own.

Victims of occupational fraud can be widespread and include families of victims as well as the families of the perpetrators. In general terms victims are much neglected, especially where there is a prosecution. Such victims are treated by the courts purely as witnesses for the prosecution. The attitude of some courts that 'no one was hurt' is in fact far from the truth. The researcher observed in many of his interviewee victims signs of emotional and psychological harm caused by the events following the discovery of occupational fraud.

Finally, a message to all my readers in business: Try not to become a victim. Be observant, and above all don't think 'It couldn't happen in my company'. I assure you that occupational fraud is rife. It can happen to any company.

Dr Brian Warrington 2014

Bibliography and sources

ACFE, (2004/2006/2010) (Association of Certified Fraud Examiners) *Report to the Nation*

ACFE Fraud Prevention Check-Up 2011
http://www.acfe.com/

On Occupational Fraud and Abuse, TX Publisher ACFE

AIS, (American Institute of Stress)
www.stress.org/americas.htm

American Heritage Dictionary of the English Language 2009, Boston, USA Houghton Mifflin

Babiak, P & Hare, R D (2006), *Snakes in Suits - when psychopaths go to work*, NY Harper Collins

Baker, J. S. (2004), *The Sociological Origins of White-collar Crime*, Washington DC. The Heritage Foundation

BCC, British Chamber of Commerce (2004) *Setting Business Free from Crime,*

London UK Pub BCC

BDO, FraudTrack 2/3/4 BDO annual fraud surveys, London

BHC (2008), Better Health Channel. Stress-Related Diabetes Australia www.betterhealth.vic.gov.au

BIG, (2008). British Institute of Graphologists, *History of Graphology UK* http://www.britishgraphology.org/

BNET Business Directory (2010) www.dictionary.bnet.com

Brock 2007 Interview with D J Brock, Assistant State Attorney, Economic Crime Unit, Florida

Britannica online, Definition Denial UK, Encyclopaedia Britannica. www.britannica.com

Buchanan-Cook, D (2006), Fraud - The Threat From Within, *UK Law Journal of Scotland*

Business Link UK, law on bullying UK http://www.businesslink.gov.uk

Campbell R, Adams A E, Wasco S M, Ahrens CE , Sefl T , (2009) *Training Interviewers for Research on Sexual Violence*, Sage.UK, http://sagepub.com

Carey, B (2007) Denial NY, *New Scientist*

Clarke J (2005), *Working with Monsters*. Sydney Australia, Random house.

Cleckley, H (1941) *The Mask of Sanity*, fifth edition 1988. Augusta Georgia. Private printing, for non-profit educational use

Cook, K S *Trust in Society*, USA New York, Russell Sage Foundation.

Comer, M (1977) *Corporate Fraud*, UK, McGraw-Hill

Companies House ND, accesses 2007. Corporate law on fraud reporting, UK Companies House

Croall, H (2001a) Understanding White-Collar Crime, UK, Open University Press

Croall, H. (2001b) *The Victims of White-Collar Crime*, L. Sven-Ake (ed), White Collar Crime Research. Old Views and Future Potentials: Lectures and Papers from a Scandinavian Seminar

National Council for Crime Prevention, Sweden Bra-Report 2001: 1. Croall, H. (2004)

Cheated and Poisoned: Exposing Victimisation from Economic Crime, Swedish Council for Crime Prevention (English summary available on www.bra.se)

Croall, H (2009) *White-Collar and Corporate Victimization*, Pamela Davies, Peter Francis and Chris Greer (Editors)

Victims Crime and Society, London, Sage

Desal, L (2004) Interview with Paul Babiak CNN online, www.cnn.com.

Dickson-Swift V, James E L, Kippen S and Liamputtong P. (2008) *Risk to Researchers in Qualitative on Sensitive Topics Research* Sage, UK, http://sagepub.com

DSM-1V (1994). *The Diagnostic Manual of the American Psychiatric Association*, US American Psychiatric Association

DTI (1971) Department of Trade and Industry Report on Pergamon Press, UK Department of Trade and Industry

DTI, (2001) Department of Trade and Industry Report on Mirror Group Newspapers plc, UK Department of Trade and Industry

Enron Trails, (2002-2006). Public knowledge; The Enron trials. US, many reports.

Fraud Act, (2006) amended 1996 chapter 62. UK, HMSO http://www.opsi.gov.uk/legislation/about_legislation

Fraud Review, (2006) UK, Her Majesty's Stationery Office

Gill, M (2005) *Learning from Fraudsters*, UK, Protiviti Ltd

Hare, R. D. (1993). *Without Conscience, The Disturbing World of the Psychopath*

Among Us. NY, Guilford Press

Hare et al, DSM -1V (1994-2000): Criticism of the DSM-1V criteria for APD US, American Psychiatric Association

HMSO, (1999) British Government White Paper, *Managing People with Severe Personality Disorder*, London UK, Her Majesty's Stationery Office

HMSO, (1968) Theft Act (1996 amendments) UK, Her Majesty's Stationery Office

ICD-10 (1992) Classification of Mental and Behaviour Disorders. Geneva, World Health Organization

Johnson B and Clarke J M (2003) *Collecting Sensitive Data: The Impact on Researchers*

Qualitative Health Research, Vol. 13 no. 3 Sage Publications UK

Jones, D. W. (2008), *Understanding Criminal Behaviour*, UK, US & Canada, Willan publishing

Karstedt, S (2007) Staff stealing survey, UK, Keele University

Kempa (2009), *Combating White-Collar Crime in Canada.*
University of Ottawa. mkemp@unottawa.ca

Kessler, M G & Associates (1999) Staff theft survey, NY
Kessler International

Kobrin, J A (2006) Annual Survey of American Law, NY New
York University.

Korsell, L (2002) Economic Crime. In crime trends in
Sweden (1988 -2000) Stockholm National Council of Crime
Prevention

KPMG, (2006/2007). Annual fraud survey, UK KPMG

KPMG, (2007): Profile of a fraudster, UK KPMG

Legal-dictionary, (2007) Definition malfeasance UK
www.legal-dictionary.thefreedictionary.com

Levi, M (1995) *Serious Fraud in Britain*, F Pearce and L
Snider (eds) Corporate Crime; Contemporary databases,
Toronto; University of Toronto Press

Levi et al (2007), *The Nature, Extent and Economic Impact of
Fraud in the UK*

UK, ACPO

McLean, B & Elkind, P (2003/04), *The Smartest Guys in the
Room.* NY Penguin Books

Norwich Union, (2004), Fraud Report, UK Norwich Union

Peninsula, staff theft survey. UK Peninsula

Piquero, N L and Benson, M L (2001) *White-collar and Criminal Careers*, Journal of Contemporary Criminal Justice

Price Waterhouse Cooper (2007), *Psychosocial Working Conditions*. UK, PWC

Price Waterhouse Cooper (2006), Fraud report, UK, PWC

Psychology Today (1994) Definition jealousy. NY Sussex Publishers LCC

Punch, M (1996), *Dirty Business: Exploring Corporate Misconduct*, London, Sage.

Rappoport, A (2005) *Co-Narcissism: How we Accommodate Narcissistic Parents* CA www.rappoport.com

Schwartz 2008, *Rape, Its Emotional Consequences*, www.mentalhelp.net

Silverman D, 2005, *Doing Qualitative Research*, second edition. Sage, London.

Stout, M (2005), *The Sociopath Next Door*, NY, Broadway Books

SFO, Serious Fraud Office (2004) UK annual report. UK, SFO

Shapiro, S (1990) *Collaring the Crime, Not the Criminal; re-considering the concept of white-collar crime*, US, American Sociological Review

Slapper, G and Tombs, S. (1999), *Corporate Crime*, London Addison-Wesley Longman

Spalek, B (2000), *White-collar Crime Victims and the Issue of Trust. The British Criminology Conference 2000, Selected*

Proceedings. Volume 4. Published 2001, UK British Society of Criminology

Stanford Encyclopaedia of Philosophy, (2002), *The Nature of Envy*, US Stanford University

Sutherland, E H (1949), *White-Collar Crime New York*: Holt, Reinhart and Winston

Sutherland, E H (1983) *White-Collar Crime, the Uncut Version*, US, Yale University

The Counseling Psychologist (1984) http://www.uk.sagepub.com

The Holy Bible, King James authorised version. Nashville, TN, World publishing

Titus and Gover ND *Crime Prevention Studies*, volume 12, pp. 133-151

Trochim (2006)
http://www.socialresearchmethods.net/kb/contents.php

UK, Mental health act (1982). Definition psychopathic disorder UK, HMSO.

Vaknin, S. (2006) *The History of Personality Disorders*, UK, BBC, www.bbc.co.uk/dna/h2g2/A13289033

Vaknin, S. (2006) *Malignant Self Love, Narcissism Revisited,* 1st edition 7th Impression. Prague & Skopje. Narcissus Publications

Victimisation from Economic Crime, Swedish Council for Crime Prevention (English summary available on www.bra.se)

Wachman, R (2005), Quoting from the Association of Certified Fraud Examiners.

UK, Observer www.observer.guardian.co.uk

Warrington B (1979-86), *Working in Canada as a Corporate Doctor*

Warrington B (2004), *Personal Experience Detecting Fraud*

Warrington B (2007), *Betrayal of Trust*
www.bcs.org/server.php?show=ConWebDoc.12930

Way I, Vandeusen KM, Martin G, Applegate B and Jandle J (2004) *Vicarious Trauma: A Comparison Of Clinicians Who Treat Survivors Of Sexual Abuse And Sexual Offenders*. Sage, UK, http://sagepub.com

Weisburd D, Waring E and Chayet, E F (2001), *White-Collar Crime and Criminal Careers*. New York: Cambridge University Press

White-collar fraud (2009);
http//www.whitecollarfraud.com/946563.html

Wysoker A 2000. *Informed Consent, the Ultimate Right*, www.apna.org

Whitecollarfraud (2009);
http//www.whitecollarfraud.co/946563.html

www.nationmaster.com/encyclopedia/Narcissus-myth#Archaic_version

Appendices

Europe uses ICD-10. Classification of Mental and behavioural Disorders.

Narcissistic Personality Disorder Traits:

Diagnostic criteria for 301.81 Narcissistic Personality Disorder: A pervasive pattern of grandiosity (in fantasy or behaviour), need for admiration and lack of empathy, beginning by early adulthood and present in a variety of contexts, as indicated by five (or more) of the following:

(1)   has a grandiose sense of self-importance (eg exaggerates achievements and talents, expects to be recognized as superior without commensurate achievements)

(2)   is preoccupied with fantasies of unlimited success, power, brilliance, beauty or ideal love

(3)   believes that he or she is special and unique and can only be understood by, or should associate with, other special or high-status people (or institutions)

(4)   requires excessive admiration

(5)   has a sense of entitlement, ie, unreasonable expectations of especially favourable treatment or automatic compliance with his or her expectations

(6)   is interpersonally exploitative, ie, takes advantage of others to achieve his or her own ends

(7)   lacks empathy: is unwilling to recognize or identify with the feelings and needs of others

(8)   is often envious of others or believes that others are envious of him or her

(9)   shows arrogant, haughty behaviours or attitudes.

APPENDIX 2

Psychopathy Checklist Revised (PCL-R)

This is a clinical rating scale with 20 items, in which both case histories and semi-structured interviews are used. Each of the items in the PCL-R is scored on a three-point (0, 1, 2) scale according to two factors. A value of 0 is assigned if the item does not apply, 1 if it applies somewhat, and 2 if it fully applies. The two factors are: emotional detachment and lifestyle. Factor One looks for a selfish, remorseless, individual with inflated self-esteem who exploits others. Factor Two describes a lifestyle that is chaotic, antisocial and/or criminal, marked by impulsiveness, a lack of responsibility and reactive anger. According to Hare, a psychopath will score high on both factors, whereas someone with Anti-Social Personality Disorder will score high only on factor two.

The items are as follows:

1.   Glibness/superficial charm

2.   Grandiose sense of self-worth

3.   Need for stimulation/proneness to boredom

4.   Pathological lying

5.   Cunning/manipulative

6.   Lack of remorse or guilt

7.   Shallow affect

8.   Callous/lack of empathy

9.   Parasitic lifestyle

10.   Poor behavioural controls

11. Promiscuous sexual behaviour

12. Early behavioural problems

13. Lack of realistic, long-term goals

14. Impulsivity

15. Irresponsibility

16. Failure to accept responsibility for own actions

17. Many short-term marital relationships

18. Juvenile delinquency

19. Revocation of conditional release

20. Criminal versatility

GLOSSARY OF TERMS

ACFE Association Of Certified Fraud Examiners.

AIS American Institute Of Stress.

BACS. Banking Automated Clearing System.

BCC British Chamber Of Commerce.

BDO BDO Stoy Hayward

BHC Better Health Channel

BIG British Institute Of Graphologists

CD ROM Compact Disk Read Only Memory

CEO Chief Executive Officer

DSM The Diagnostic Manual of the American Psychiatric Association

DTI Department Of Trade And Industry, UK

FBI Federal Bureau of Investigation, US

FD Finance Director

HMSO Her Majesty's Stationery Office, UK

ICD-10 Classification of Mental and Behaviour Disorders. (World Health Organisation)

KPMG Klinveld Peat Marwick Goerdeler

MD Managing director

NCIS National Criminal Investigation Service

NU Norwich Union, UK

OF Occupational Fraud. The use of an employee's occupation for personal gain. Planned embezzlement and the falsifying of company records to cover up stealing of assets and or money. Not to be confused with occupational stealing which is opportunistic.

PWC Price Waterhouse Cooper

SAGE Sage is a suite of business software that is packed with specialist modules to help organizations with a typical turnover of £1m-£20m

SFO Serious Fraud Office UK

WCC White-collar Crime. Within the field of criminology white-collar crime has been defined by Edwin Sutherland as a crime committed by a person of respectability and high social status in the course of his occupation (Sutherland 1949).